Understanding your car

Roy Johnstone

Macdonald Guidelines

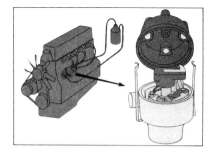

© Macdonald Educational Ltd. 1977
First published 1977
Macdonald Educational Ltd.
Holywell House,
Worship Street,
London EC2A 2EN

Made and printed by
Waterlow (Dunstable) Ltd.

ISBN 0 356 060160

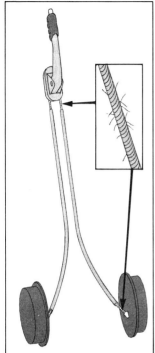

Contents

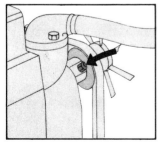

Introduction

Car manufacturers take great pains to point out to the potential car buyer how various and wonderful are the refinements in their latest models. The array of gadgetry is designed to impress and lure customers. It succeeds.

Whether it is intended to give the impression that such sophistication is fresh out of today's think tanks, the powerful way the message is put across in the glossy mass-media advertisements and on street hoardings, the consumer can be forgiven for thinking that the emphasized selling features are brand-new ideas. In fact, nothing is further from the truth. The caption opposite pinpoints the years when the trimmings were first introduced.

Such embellishments as those mentioned opposite tend to obscure the fact that much current research is directed towards the development of new methods of propulsion. This change in priority has been brought about by the world crisis in the oil market, just as, in the 19th century, the internal combustion engine was initially developed to provide a more efficient, less awkward, faster and lighter power source than steam.

In the early days, especially in Britain, obstructions marked every stage of the motor car's progress: in 1865, would-be motorists had to face extortionate road tolls, a speed limit of 2 mph in towns (which was strictly enforced), and provide each vehicle with three drivers, one of whom had to walk in front. Nowadays, devotees of the horseless carriage almost everywhere have to contend with high parking charges and taxation, together with protests from all sides against pollution caused by motor vehicles and the introduction of major road schemes likely to destroy the character of our surroundings.

Motoring for the few

As costs spiral and world inflation depletes individual incomes, there is also every possibility that motoring could revert to its original status—that of a luxury for the wealthy minority. Indeed, it can be argued that many motorists would not be on the road now were it not for the fact that they are driving company cars. For many others, who own the vehicles they drive, it is becoming ever clearer that they will only continue to motor on by taking stringent economies. For this reason, a major part of this book will be devoted to simple tasks that even the least handy of drivers can carry out in order to reduce significantly the cost of running a car in the 1970s.

▼In 1899 Dion Bouton presented its first 'vis-à-vis' with a one cylinder 3.5hp engine.

Nothing's new

Don't be fooled by the publicity campaigns. Much of the sophisticated gadgetry on today's cars is not as new as manufacturers would like you to believe.

Since the '60s, for instance, a lot of thought has been put into electric cars. Yet these were all the rage from 1881 until 1910. The first V4 engine was built not in the second half of the 20th century, but in France in 1897. Direct fuel injection, another popular 'extra' of late, was patented in 1902 by Amédée Bollée. In the same year British inventor, Dr Frederick Lanchester, designed the disc brake. As for automatic transmission, remarkable as it might seem, this first appeared in the USA in 1904. Also in America in 1904, the Cadillac company offered anti-theft ignition locks as an option. The idea of a transversely-mounted, front-wheel drive engine was first used in America in 1909. Servo-assisted brakes? These have had numerous mentions in recent car advertisements, too. They were actually introduced by Hispano-Suiza in 1919. Other revived inventions — automatic reversing lamp: 1921, adjustable steering column: 1923, body rustproofing: 1929, windscreen washers: 1937, two-speed wipers: 1940, radial tyres: 1948, tinted glass: 1950, power steering: 1951, twin headlamps: 1954.

Development 1860-1901

The motor car was a twinkle in man's eye as far back as the 13th century. A distinguished scholar of the time, Roger Bacon, predicted: 'One day we shall endow chariots with incredible speed without the aid of any animal.'

Inventors tried to realize the dream in many different ways, using mobile windmills, giant clockwork motors, steam propulsion and, once the principles were mastered, electricity. Even gunpowder was considered a possible means of making man mobile.

Strangely, it was this last idea that gave birth to the internal combustion engine. In 1678 the theory was propounded that a piston could be made to move in a cylinder by the force of a gunpowder explosion. More than a century later a Swiss engineer,

▲ Carl Benz, the German-born inventor, not only created what is acknowledged as the first true car, but was also the first to produce a petrol-driven car in any quantity – the 2¾hp Benz 'Velo' of 1894.

▼ The world's first practical petrol-burning vehicle: Carl Benz's three-wheeler of 1885. Despite the revolution it was to cause, it drew little attention at the start.

De Rivaz, successfully built a crude vehicle on these lines in which explosive gases were ignited by a device called a Volta's gun.

Further experiments involved household gas, but it was not until the advent of a suitable liquid fuel, during the period 1820-50, that real progress could be made. In 1885 a German, Carl Benz, constructed the world's first *practical* petrol-burning car. Its engine is described on page 19.

Six years later another German, Wilhelm Maybach, designed the Mercedes for Daimler. This, with its pressed steel chassis and its engine mounted ahead of the passenger compartment under a characteristic bonnet, was the true forerunner of the modern car.

Steam and electric car heyday

Even so, the ghost of steam propulsion was not to be laid for a while yet. In 1888 the renaissance of the 'flash' boiler by the French engineer Leon Serpollet helped to popularize steam cars and make them safer. In the 'flash' boiler, a series of tubes was kept extremely hot so that small amounts of water pumped into them were instantly converted into high-pressure superheated steam. This in turn was fed into cylinders, where the force exerted by the steam caused the pistons to move. This type of boiler was far less likely to burst because the tubes were designed to withstand enormous pressure, and steam was generated only as required.

Eight years later Serpollet changed from coke-burning to paraffin and, three years after that, succeeded in simplifying lubrication.

In 1897 the American Stanley brothers produced the Locomobile, a steam vehicle that flourished in England and the USA and was widely imitated into the 1900s. Its petrol-fired furnace heated a vertical boiler at the rear, and a simple tubular frame supported a two-seater buggy. The Locomobile consumed about a gallon of water per mile, and used more petrol than its internal-combustion counterparts.

Electric cars were also in vogue at the end of the 19th century following the development of the DC motor and the heavy, bulky lead-acid battery. Their one big drawback was range; despite this, however, they were especially popular with women as town runabouts—particularly in America where, in 1891, the Electric Road Carriage Co. of Boston became the world's first manufacturers of electric cars for private use. Electric racing cars, too, made a name for themselves; indeed, in 1899, the famous driver Camille Jenatzy broke the world flying kilometre record with an astonishing 105.904 kph in his cigar-shaped *Jamais Contente*.

Today, the widely forecast reintroduction of electric cars has been delayed by the fundamental problem of range. It seems that modern research has achieved very little in view of the fact that in 1891, William Morris of Iowa recorded a continuous run of 13 hours at slightly under 15 mph.

It was against this background of steam and electric impracticability that the inter-

▶ A French electric cab of 1889. The driver was perched precariously at the back and overlooked the roof.

nal combustion engine blossomed. However, although the basic principles of much of the early pioneer work have remained a subject of reappraisal to this day, we do seem to have overcome the primary headache of the early years—physically operating and controlling the machinery.

The joys of motoring

Woe betide the pioneer driver if his car began to roll backwards downhill because the going was too steep or the vehicle had broken down. Brakes were usually pedal-operated bands which in forward travel wrapped round a drum on the drive shaft. In reverse, they unwrapped. This meant that the motorist had to steer smartly into the kerb or a hedge to avoid catastrophe.

Keeping a car going was a fraught activity, too. The Bunsen burners, for instance, which were the heat source for the hot-tube ignition system, had an unnerving habit of being extinguished by the wind. Without their vital supply of heat, the platinum tube could not be maintained at the very high temperature necessary to ignite the petrol-air mixture in the cylinder at each compression stroke.

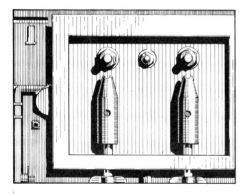

▲ Hot-tube ignition system.

▶ Chain drive.

Carburettors

The mixing of petrol and air took place in the surface vapourizer carburettors until the end of the 19th century which, to add to the driver's problems, had an extra air control. This had to be adjusted when the throttle valve, which controlled the opening of the pipe leading to the engine, was substantially altered. This adjustment effectively determined the mixture strength. A horizontal plate (1) spread incoming air over the fuel surface; evaporation was increased by a pipe heated by the exhaust (2).

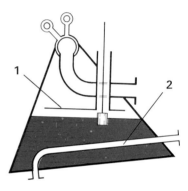

Early transmission systems

The engine turned the roadwheels by belt at first, then by chain. In 1899 the French

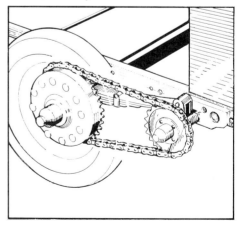

▲ The Daimler Cannstatt of 1895, built in Germany and Britain. It had a 1500cc two-cylinder 'V' engine. Its ignition system was an externally heated platinum tube.

manufacturer, Renault, devised today's system of a propeller shaft (with universal joint) driving a bevel pinion meshed with a crown wheel carrying a differential on the rear axle.

Four years earlier another French engineer, Emile Levassor, put the change-speed gears in a protective box and, for good measure, adapted the cone clutch for car use (see right). By releasing the clutch ring (1), the driven cone (2), to which the gear shaft was attached, was uncoupled from the driving cone (3) and crankshaft. Previously, to change gear, engine disengagement was accomplished by manoeuvring a belt onto fast and loose pulleys.

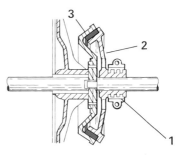

Development 1902-1939

Undoubtedly the most influential event this century in the development of the motor car was the introduction of mass production by Henry Ford at Detroit in 1908. Cars had now also assumed their own identity—they were no longer just motorized carriages.

Following its inception in 1895, the pneumatic tyre, too, had become standard, and Panhard and Renault set a lead by offering complete weather protection.

Radiators had also become commonplace, steering wheels had replaced tillers, and the 'gate' gear change was becoming established. So was the foot accelerator, which had superseded hand control.

Meanwhile, the English engineer Frederick Lanchester had radically improved engine lubrication with a pumped

▼ True to his promise that 'I will build a car for the great multitudes', Henry Ford set up the world's first true assembly line and, with that, mass production was born. In scarcely any time at all, Ford's empire stretched half across the world.

high-pressure system (he was also a pioneer of mechanically-operated engine valves), while the French aristocrat Count Albert de Dion, in partnership with Georges Bouton, was behind two major advances—a rear axle which allowed almost all the weight of the final drive gear to be sprung, and precisely machined parts which led to high-speed engines that were also more efficient. As vehicle speeds rose, brakes came under closer scrutiny. The main snags were that the crude lining materials of the day had a habit of burning out on steep descents, and that the systems—which only acted on the rear wheels in the manner of bicycle and horse-drawn carriage brakes—couldn't cope if a car rolled backwards. To prevent breakaways, vehicles were fitted with special anchor devices that, when released, dug into the road surface.

It was at this time that the first disc brake was patented by Lanchester but, like so many early ideas, it was another 50 years before it was developed. A year later in 1903, however, came the forerunner of the

conventional brake drum, and five years after that, linings made of asbestos, solidified in high melting point resins. Even so, it wasn't until the introduction of four-wheel braking in 1911—the year the electric starter motor made its debut—that stopping power really improved. Hydraulic brakes followed nine years later (eight years before the advent of synchromesh gears). The '20s and early '30s will always be remembered as the age of elegance—an era that produced styling which to this day has never been surpassed. In contrast, but of equal historical importance, was the start of a modern-day success story—the appearance in 1938 of the Nazi-inspired Volkswagen. Compactness and economy became very much the dictates in the '30s as a result of the Slump. It was clear that, with money increasingly hard to come by, the last thing the majority wanted was to pay

▲ If you want to be noticed, be seen in a car' would seem to be the soft-sell message of this early De Dion Bouton poster.

▼ One Nazi legacy for which the world can be grateful: the record-breaking Volkswagen Beetle here being launched by Hitler in 1938.

highly for large, luxurious models that gulped petrol. And so mass production became the manufacturers' by-word for survival, bringing with it a big swing to smart, low-priced family saloons.

The ignition system

With so much development and change it is perhaps scarcely surprising that many 'advances' came about through the re-vamping of old ideas. Ignition systems are one example. The conventional type in current use owes its origins to Georges Bouton, who was working on ignition methods at the turn of the century, but its potential was not at first realized. As a result, magneto ignition became standard.

In the magneto ignition system power was generated by a primary winding of

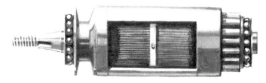

▼ Magnetos were the hub of car ignitions. Pictured is the complete armature.

thick wire revolving inside magnets. On top of this wire, separated by an insulator, was a second winding of much thinner wire and at least 50 times more of it. The second winding's job was to intensify the charge, and it was this current that provided the ignition spark. A condenser was fitted to suppress an otherwise destructive spark at the contacts.

The component that made this possible

Although pneumatic tyres were invented in 1845, it wasn't for another 50 years that they were fitted to a car for the first time – when Edouard Michelin used some he had designed in the Paris-Bordeaux race that year.

Eight years later, Christian Gray and Thomas Sloper improved on an earlier invention by making a tyre incorporating complete plies of diagonal cords. This became known as the cross-ply.

In 1913, Gray and Sloper came up with a design in which the cords were set radially, with circumferential belts of fabric or wire. This idea wasn't exploited for another 45 years. When the Michelin company did so with steel belts, the radial tyre was born.

Pneumatic tyre shapes

changed drastically in 1904 when the Caoutchouc and Michelin firms produced flat raised treads which provided more grip than the smooth rounded tyres of the day.

These early types had inner tubes, of course, and it's interesting to recall three of the designs. One, the predecessor of the tube still around today, was actually sausage-shaped with blank ends – designed to make the business of threading it back under the outer cover easier after a puncture repair. The next step was to fasten the two ends together with hooks and eyes. This was superseded by a connection that depended on the air pressure for its tightness, but at least gave an air cushion all the way round.

For information on modern-day tyres, see page 89.

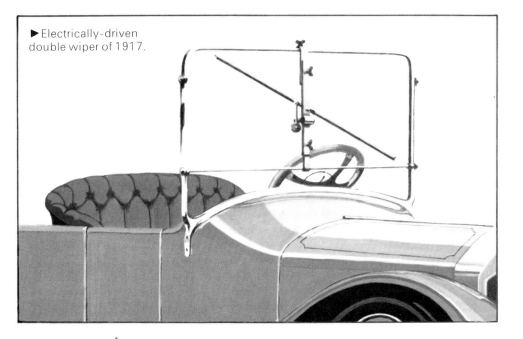

► Electrically-driven double wiper of 1917.

was the contact 'make-and-break'. This completed the primary circuit to enable the initial current to be developed, then broke it to allow the high voltage charge to be generated in the second winding. The action was achieved by a contact on the rotating windings (the armature) striking two fixed cams, each of which united and separated two pieces of platinum. The make-and-break occurred twice per revolution.

The current was fed to a rotor arm revolving in the distributor at half the armature's speed. Each time the carbon brush on this arm came in contact with the equi-distant metal strips on a fixed ring the charge was transmitted to the appropriate sparking plug.

(Today, current from a battery is intensified by a coil, and the rotor arm is in the distributor driven off the engine camshaft.)

Windscreen wipers and heaters

Electric windscreen wipers were introduced in 1917, with a blade that moved see-saw fashion, while heating systems—surprisingly—have been in existence since 1905. Early types were floor-mounted tanks, through which the hot exhaust gases were diverted.

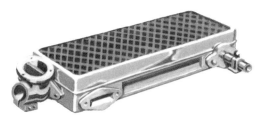

▲ Exhaust heating device or foot-warmer, designed to be fitted in the floor of a car.

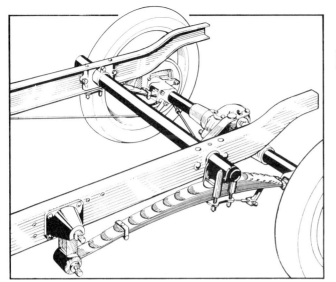

▲ The auxiliary device that absorbed minor vibrations.

◀ An early suspension system with a movable cross-member.

Suspension

The main contributions to comfort, however, were suspension improvements. At the turn of the century, most cars were fitted only with rigid cart springs. Comfort was rapidly improved with the advent of the shock absorber: today's familiar telescopic device, in which a piston moves in a cylinder against the resistance offered by an oil, actually dates back to 1901.

But at the turn of the century, and indeed, for some years afterwards, a number of suspension systems were employed. One, the Hartford damper, used a friction material between four discs, and could be adjusted by means of a centre nut. The snag was that it was relatively insensitive to the amount of spring movement.

Another popular method of shock absorption, invented in the mid '20s, was the Gabriel snubber. This consisted of a flexible strap wound several times round two movable members, in between which was placed a compression spring. Initial upward spring movement was undamped, but the return downward motion was retarded as the strap tightened round the sprung core.

Carburettors

Carburettors changed drastically, too. In the 1914 Zenith model (shown), fuel was supplied through two jets (1 and 2) which were so arranged that they accurately apportioned petrol flow to air flow according to the engine suction. When the petrol level was correct—about 2mm ($\frac{1}{16}$ in) below the jet orifices—fuel supply was automatically shut off by a needle valve (3) when the float (4) pushed against weights on toggle levers (5).

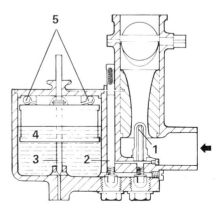

Development 1945-today

If the period before World War II was the *real* age of technical development, the years since have been a time for refinement—and for the increasingly severe restrictions imposed upon manufacturers by legislators, environmentalists, accountants and the oil crisis.

Development was slow in Europe after the end of the war owing to rebuilding and retooling programmes, and steel shortages. Another problem was that until high-octane petrol became available, production of the new breed of high-compression engines could not begin.

When production finally started in earnest, the design emphasis was on functional requirement. Independent front suspension allowed engine and passenger compartments to be placed lower and further forward, improving road-holding, passenger comfort and the capacities of luggage boots at the rear. Further lowering was achieved by running the propeller shaft below the centre line of the crown wheel.

Safety improved, too, with the introduction in 1948 of tubeless tyres, which significantly reduced the blow-out risk. Five years later, radial tyres were introduced and their greater flexibility and wider area of contact with the road not only had an extremely beneficial effect on roadholding, but also on owners' pockets, for they last much longer than cross-plys. (More recently, the appearance of squatter shaped tyres has led to even better stability, particularly when cornering.)

Manufacturers' preoccupation with cost-cutting brought greater use of plastics and wide-scale adoption of monocoque construction, which dispensed with the chassis.

Italian genius

Two significant advances came in 1959. Both were masterstrokes of Italian designers and put into production by the then British Motor Corporation. In order of importance they were the Austin Morris Mini (created by Sir Alec Issigonis) and the Austin A40 Countryman, conceived by Pininfarina.

The Mini concept—a small economy car seating four adults—is still being used by practically every European maker. Issigonis, providing an effective, timely answer to the bubble-car challenge, made the best of his "baby's" sparse dimensions by fitting a front-wheel-drive transverse engine and slotting the gearbox underneath it.

The Austin A40, according to its publicity, was "the car that all others have led up to". In fact, time has shown that it was "the car that has led up to all others". For the Countryman version, with its third door at the back, was the first of a breed that today has become a major fashion—the hatchback.

▼ With their low fuel consumption, bubble cars like this German Messerschmitt were immensely popular in the 1950s.

Unhappily, the fortunes of the British company (now Leyland Cars) have waned, but those of Italian designers have never been better. Pininfarina, Giugaro, Bertone and Ghia are all Italian, and responsible for the styling of Europe's top-selling cars. Couple this with standardization processes born out of international safety legislation and market research, and you have the reason why so many makes and models look alike. Ironically the soaring costs of motor fuel have encouraged designers to reconsider electric and even steam propulsion again.

A major step forward has been electronic ignition—a necessity for 8- and 12-cylinder engines because it is difficult for conventional contact points systems to provide the number of sparks per second needed. It has the added advantages of being more reliable, whatever the car, and maintenance-free. Future development will incorp-

◄ The car that was ahead of its time — the Austin A40. Its manufacturer hasn't produced a 'hatchback' in Britain since.

▼ Hatchback — 1976 Volvo-style. This 343 model, made in Holland, is one of the latest cars to follow the European 'third door' trend.

343 DL

▶ The original Mini. This masterstroke of Sir Alec Issigonis has been followed by nearly every European manufacturer. Introduced in 1959, it is still being made in Britain, though it is due to be superseded soon. In fact, British Leyland's now-closed Italian factory brought out a completely new hatchback Mini called the Innocenti in 1974. The Mini was truly the first small family car with unprecedented roadholding and spaciousness; it was also economical on fuel.

orate mini-computers, leading to fuel-saving, improved performance and reduction of exhaust levels.

The alternator—another recent innovation—is gradually superseding the dynamo. Its main benefits are that it produces more current to charge the battery even when idling, needs less maintenance and is more reliable. The major difference (apart from the fact that one delivers DC, the other AC) is that a dynamo's generating windings rotate whereas the alternator's, being outside the armature, are stationary. They do have one feature in common, however: both are fanbelt-driven.

Oil, brake, headlamp, steering and heating/ventilation performances have also been improved. Advances in motor oil technology have culminated in an engine lubricant which, a three-month independent trial has concluded, actually brings

about an average fuel saving of 6.8 per cent. This is BP's VF7—a much thinner oil than rival products—to which secret additives have been mixed to provide adequate protection of modern-day engines.

The advent of disc brakes, too, has revolutionized motoring. First offered by Citroën in 1955 as standard equipment on the DS19 model exactly 53 years after Dr Frederick Lanchester patented the concept,

▶ You could get three Ford Comutas in one parking meter space . . . yet each one would seat two adults and three children. But it will be some while yet before electric cars become a practical proposition.

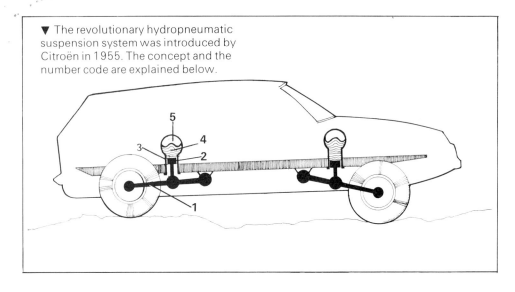

▼ The revolutionary hydropneumatic suspension system was introduced by Citroën in 1955. The concept and the number code are explained below.

many manufacturers have since followed suit, fitting them at least to the front wheels.

The main advantage of disc brakes is that they can be cooled efficiently—an important consideration as speeds have risen and braking has inevitably become harder. This in turn has subjected systems to intense heat, causing fading of efficiency. Another improvement has been the development of brake anti-lock mechanisms.

Hydropneumatic suspension

Among outstanding post-war developments has been the Citroën-inspired independent hydropneumatic suspension. Each wheel is attached to the structure by an arm (1) connected to a piston (2) that slides in a cylinder (3) against the twin resistances of fluid (4) and nitrogen (5); the method also ensures a minimum ground clearance.

The Denovo tyre

Tyre technology has culminated in the Dunlop Denovo, which enables drivers to retain control even in 70-mph blowouts,

and continue for another hundred miles at up to 50 mph without changing the wheel.

The "secret" is a lubricant which, automatically released from interior dispensers, prevents disintegration through heat build-up, seals the puncture and slightly inflates the tyre; a specially-designed wheel rim does the rest.

▼ The Denovo tyre.

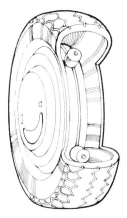

How it works

What goes on under the bonnet of most cars today is not so different from what went on in the Benz engine of 1885. The German inventor even employed electric ignition through a generator, battery and sparking plug (1). The spark was turned on and off by a device not unlike a domestic doorbell mechanism.

The inlet valve (2) fed carburated fuel from a surface vapourizer into the cylinder (3) which, when ignited, caused the piston (4) to move and turn the vertical crankshaft (5). This drove the flywheel (6) and, through bevel pinion gearing (7), a short horizontal shaft at half the speed of the crankshaft (the forerunner of today's camshaft).

Connected to this shaft were rods that operated the fuel inlet valve and exhaust outlet valve (8), the gases being ejected through (9). The horizontal shaft also turned the pulley (10), which transmitted power to the motion shaft by belt. From here the back wheels were turned by chains and sprockets. The engine, which had to be push-started, was water-cooled via the "radiator" (11).

Benz's four-stroke engine developed 0.8 horsepower at 250 revolutions per minute. Its most unusual feature was the horizontally-mounted flywheel—Benz was convinced that vertical mounting would make cornering difficult because of gyroscopic action.

His path to fame certainly wasn't smooth. Six years after co-founding an engineering company with money from an advanced dowry, bankruptcy stared him in the face. But he survived and he finished his first car in 1885—only for it to crash into a wall on its first test.

After a number of early snags had been solved, a sturdier version of the three-wheeler emerged in 1898. But there were few takers. In the 1890s, however, his four-wheeled "Velo" made him the most successful manufacturer of his time.

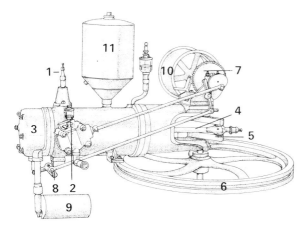

◄ When Carl Benz patented his first petrol-driven car in 1886, he described it as a 'vehicle propelled by a gas engine, the fuel for which consists of gas vapourized from a liquid by means of an apparatus carried on the vehicle'. On its first road trial, the car reached 9mph.

The four-stroke engine

Operation of a conventional modern front mounted four-stroke, four-cylinder engine: the choke cable (1) closes a flap in the carburettor (2) which, by reducing the air flow, produces a rich fuel mixture. On some cars this is done automatically.
Through a solenoid relay (4) the starter switch — operated by the ignition key (3) —sends a heavy current to the starter motor (5) which turns the flywheel and the crankshaft (6) connected to it. At this stage, the crankshaft moves the pistons up and down in the cylinders, and, by means of a chain or belt, drives a camshaft (7) (see bottom right) which moves the

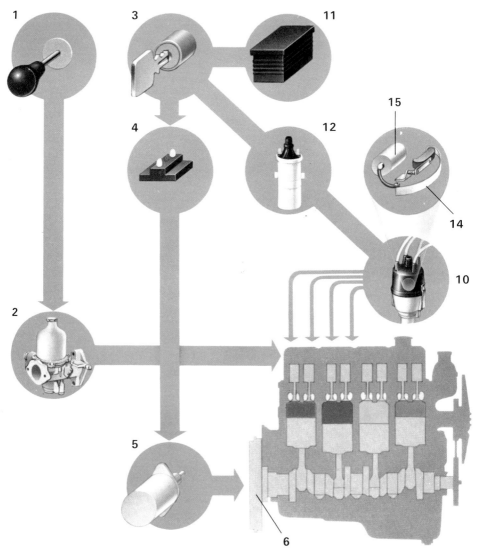

push rods (8) in a reciprocating (up and down) motion. These in turn open and shut the inlet valves (9) that admit the fuel vapour into each cylinder during the downward motion cycle of the relevant piston. This is called the induction stroke. The camshaft also drives the rotor arm in the distributor (10). When this lines up with each of the four distributor points, current from the battery (11) —transformed by the coil (12) from 12 to thousands of volts—is passed to the appropriate sparking plug (13). Additionally in the distributor are the contact breaker points (14), also driven from the camshaft which, on opening, cause the coil to produce the high voltage. A condenser (15) is fitted to prevent burning of the contact breaker points. The fuel mixture compressed during the upward motion of the piston, (the compression stroke) is ignited by the ensuing spark and the resulting explosion and air expansion force the piston down. This, the power stroke, gives the crankshaft momentum. As the piston moves upwards again (the exhaust stroke), the spent gases are expelled through another valve (16) connected to the camshaft. Once the engine fires, the starter motor cuts out automatically. To keep the crankshaft in balance, the cylinder firing order is: 1, 3, 4, 2, or 1, 2, 4, 3.

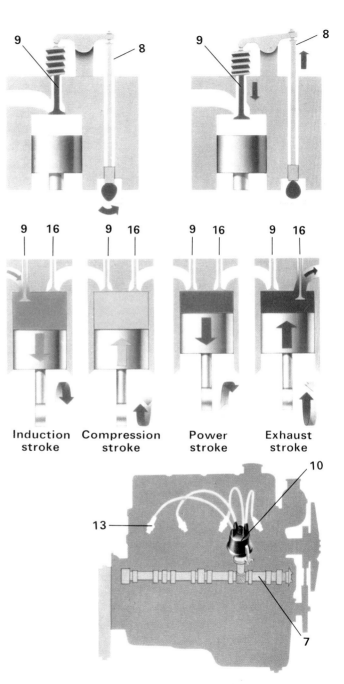

Induction stroke   Compression stroke   Power stroke   Exhaust stroke

The clutch

Depressing the foot pedal forces the clutch plate from

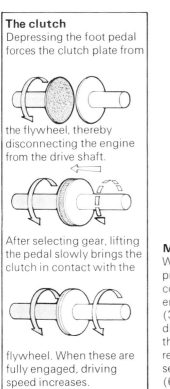

the flywheel, thereby disconnecting the engine from the drive shaft.

After selecting gear, lifting the pedal slowly brings the clutch in contact with the

flywheel. When these are fully engaged, driving speed increases.

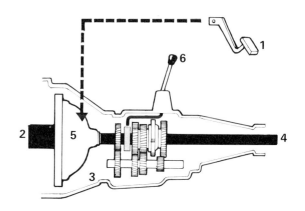

Manual gearbox

When changing gear, pressure on pedal (1) disconnects power from the engine (2) to the gearbox (3) and drive shaft (4) by disengaging the clutch from the flywheel at (5). The required gear is then selected by moving the lever (6) into the appropriate notch. This brings certain gearwheels into contact in the gearbox. To obtain a low ratio (fast engine revs, but a slow driving speed), a small gear is made to drive a larger gear. A high ratio is induced by a large gear driving a smaller gear. A special wheel called an idler is so arranged that a reverse drive motion is produced.

Lubrication

With so many moving parts, most turning at thousands of revolutions a minute, engine lubrication is vital. Without it, everything would seize up through the intense heat caused by the friction of metal continually coming into contact with metal.

To ensure trouble-free running, a pump —driven by the crankshaft or camshaft— forces oil in the sump through pipes and passages to the mechanisms, the most important of which are the camshaft, rocker arm and crankshaft bearings. Among these are the big ends which allow the pistons to turn the crankshaft smoothly.

The oil is pumped through a filter to remove impurities and, after flowing round the engine, is returned to the sump for re-use. The cylinder walls, the valve gear and the tappets (which transfer movement from the camshaft to the push rods activating the valve gear via a rocker arm shaft) are also fed this way.

Cooling

Because of the intense heat caused by combustion, it is necessary to cool things down and, in the majority of cars, a pump driven by the fanbelt circulates water through passages around the interior of the cylinder block and head.

The coolant enters at the bottom and, by the time it flows out through the top, it is very hot. To reduce the temperature ready for re-cycling, the water passes through the radiator where it is cooled by fresh air

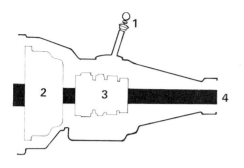

Automatic gearbox

The hub of this system is a governor activated by road speed. At low road speed it offers little resistance, allowing the throttle to move a valve which supplies oil pressure to the low gear selector. At high speed, the governor exerts sufficient resistance to send pressure to the high gear selector. There is no clutch pedal, but a lever often offers up to 6 selector positions: P (Park), R (Reverse), N (Neutral), D (Forward Drive), and 1st and 2nd gear retentions for maximum engine braking. A sharp kick-down on the throttle induces a lower gear ratio for extra acceleration.

1. Gear lever.
2. Clutch.
3. Automatic gearbox.
4. Drive-shaft.

sucked in by the fan.

A separate route carries hot water to another radiator which provides warmth to the passenger compartment.

Transmission

As explained in the diagrams above, the roadwheels are turned by way of the gearbox and propshaft. Some cars also have overdrive—an additional gear independent of the gearbox and fitted behind it. This is operated by a switch on the gear selector lever, and the high ratio obtained enables the engine to run slower and therefore more economically yet produce the same road speeds normally achieved in top, or both third and fourth gears.

The final stage of the transmission on conventional drive cars is the rear axle, differential and half-shaft assembly. A small-toothed gear (the pinion) at the end of the propshaft is meshed with a much larger gear, the crownwheel, set at right angles to it.

The half-shafts, attached to the roadwheels, are not joined directly to the crownwheel but through a differential gear. This enables them to run at the same speed when the car is travelling straight but at different revolutions when going round bends; this is because the wheel on the outside has to travel faster and further than its partner during cornering.

▼ Section of the differential showing the crownwheel and pinion.

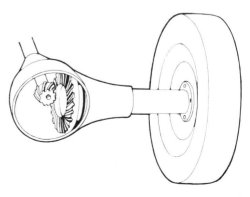

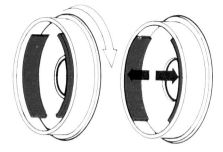

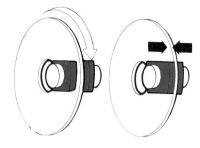

Drum brakes

When the foot pedal is depressed, fluid pressure in the slave cylinders operates pistons that force the brakes against the insides of the drums which revolve with the wheels. Where drums are fitted all round, each front wheel brake normally has two slave cylinders (one for each shoe).

Disc brakes

The disc system exerts a more powerful braking effect. In this method, hydraulic pressure forces friction pads against the side surfaces of a revolving steel disc. A big advantage with this system is that, unlike drums, only a small part of the disc is in contact with the pads at any one time, allowing more efficient cooling.

Suspension

Both the rear axle and rear wheels are suspended on a long curved spring assembly on each side. On the front wheels, the springs are usually coil-shaped. The springs help to keep the car body steady even when the wheels are moving up and down with the bumps in the road; the suspension is completed by shock absorbers or spring dampers which restrict this bouncing movement for increased road-holding stability and passenger comfort.

Engine designs

There are a number of suspension assembly variations, some of which are shown later. And like many other systems on the car, there are several kinds of engine designs—the number and arrangement of the cylinders, for instance. There are 4-, 6-, 8- and 12-cylinder types, while layouts range from the four-in-line shown on pages 20-21 to the horizontally opposed flat four and "V" styles, among others. In addition, some

engines have overhead camshafts which directly operate the valves, whilst East Germany still produces two-stroke cars with three cylinders which run on a petrol-oil mixture. Another variation is the rotary engine in which the piston rotates in the cylinder rather than moving up and down. These are dwindling in popularity now because of their high fuel consumption. The VW Beetle, on the other hand, is a rear-engine, rear-wheel drive car, whereas the Mini has a front-engine, front-wheel drive with the engine mounted transversely. Both these cars have direct transmission which eliminates the propshaft.

The brakes

Operation of the most important mechanism of all—the brakes—is described in the diagrams above. The reason hydraulic systems are favoured is that, once force is applied by the appropriate foot pedal, fluid pressure is exactly the same throughout the system. In turn, this ensures that the brakes

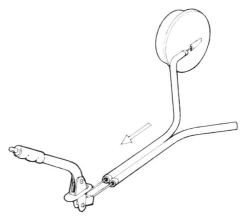

Hydraulic system

The footbrake pedal pushes a piston in the master cylinder (2). This compresses the fluid in the whole system, and the extra pressure activates the slave cylinder (3) on the stationary backplates of the wheels. When the backplate is released, the master cylinder is reconnected to a reservoir (1) which automatically replenishes any small fluid loss. A special valve maintains slight pressure in the system to prevent air from entering.

on all four road-wheels are activated simultaneously. That is, providing the circulation is totally free of air, water, contamination and leaks.

Because the car's weight is thrown forwards in a braking situation, the system is designed so that the front wheels exert a greater brake effort than those on the rear. This is achieved by fitting larger pistons in the front slave cylinders which effectively increase the pressure at these points.

On some models, check valves prevent pressure exceeding a pre-determined amount, thus avoiding wheel lock and skidding. A number of cars, too, are fitted with servo mechanisms which draw vacuum from the engine and lessen the physical effort required to operate the footbrake pedal.

Another fairly common feature is dual-braking, which has two independent circuits so that if one fails the other still provides half the braking effort.

The handbrake

The handbrake, by law, must be applied whenever the car is parked. Operation of the lever pulls a cable or rod assembly, the other end of which is connected to the rear brakes—either directly (see below), or indirectly via a swivel device.

Society and the car

Most motorists today think that, considering the cost of petrol, the weight of restrictive legislation affecting them and so on, theirs is not an easy load to bear. They should, nonetheless, be grateful that they were not living in England before the turn of the century. Strangely, the very nation that had given birth to railways and sparked off the Industrial Revolution was vehemently against cars when the 'infernal' internal-combustion machine first clattered into earshot.

It is even stranger to recall that motor spirit—the very essence that made possible the car as we know it today—was a British discovery. First, in the 1820s, Michael Faraday extracted benzine from coal tar. Then, thirty years later, the oil industry was born—not in America, as is often thought, but in Scotland, where the Glasgow chemist Dr James Young succeeded in producing oil from his country's oil shales.

Yet it was not until 1897, twelve years after Carl Benz had given the world its first practical petrol-driven car, that an English motoring engineer made any real contribution to technical expertise. He was Frederick Lanchester who, in his 2-cylinder model of that year, embodied a shaft drive in preference to chain-and-belt transmission, a worm-geared rear axle, and a fully-balanced engine with two contra-rotating crankshafts to reduce noise.

Just how far Britain was behind the Germans and the French can be gauged by the fact that, in 1895, there were only half a dozen motor vehicles actually in use in the UK. It was small wonder that British motoring got off to such a slow start.

The long-suffering motorist

A parliamentary Act passed 24 years previously stipulated that drivers of mechanical contraptions were required to pay up to 13 times more in road tolls than drivers of horse-drawn traffic. In addition to this anomaly, county authorities could exact a licence fee of £10 from vehicles entering their boundaries. As if that were not all, a

▼ Preceded by a man with a red flag C. S. Rolls drives his first motor car: a 3.7hp Peugeot made in 1896, the same year the Red Flag Act was abolished.

▼ Doctors were quick to realize the benefits of the motor car. Here, a GP is chauffeured in a Peugeot.

▲ The gate-keeper exacts her sixpenny toll from a motorist at the turn of the century. The money would go towards the upkeep of the road.

▲ The Stratford Turnpike in America. The appearance of turnpikes has changed dramatically since 1900, but their purpose is the same.

further Act in 1865 decreed that each mechanical carriage should carry at least three people capable of driving it, one of whom had to precede the 'locomotive' on foot by not less than 60 yards displaying a red flag. Worse, the maximum speeds permitted were 4 mph in the country and 2 mph in towns and villages. Penalties for offenders were severe.

It was not until 1896 that officialdom began to take a more tolerant view and, that year, the speed limit was raised to 14 mph — a joyous event celebrated by pioneer stalwarts with an emancipation run from London to Brighton, which continues to be held annually with veteran cars to this day.

Meanwhile the public, too, had started to accept the "monster" after protesting for years about the dust it stirred up on the bad, inadequate roads, and the noise that terrified livestock. Even so, the car's increase in popularity was slow. In 1899, for example, there were only 33 petrol stockists in the whole of Britain.

The real turning-point proved to be the 1000-mile Automobile Club trial of 1900, in

which 65 vehicles participated, and which gave many people their first view of the car. After that, car sales increased — though only the really wealthy could afford them.

In contrast, there was no heavy-handed legislation in the early days on the Continent. Indeed, such was the interest in the car in mainland Europe that, while the British faced crippling restrictions, France, in 1894, organized the world's first motor race.

Getting into gear

However, the motoring scene on the Continent and in Britain did have one

▶ One reason the early motorist was so unpopular with the public was that he left clouds of dust in his wake.

▲ Poor roads made pumping up tyres a regular chore.

▶ Dust prevention experiments in 1907.

common feature—discomfort. This had a marked influence on fashion. By necessity the emphasis had to be on protection simply because cars were totally open to the weather; there were no windscreens, no built-up sides and no roofs.

To combat the appalling clouds of dust, showers of rain and mud and the cold, goggles, peaked caps, scarves, hoods, heavy wraps and even thick brown paper were the inelegant order of the day.

Roads

Development of roads in the 19th century had been severely delayed by the great railway and canal bonanza but, thanks to civil engineers such as Thomas Telford and Loudon MacAdam, there were some improvements, although in Britain these were largely restricted to parts of major routes. Telford favoured the use of large stones for the foundation with smaller stones on top. MacAdam's formula was to use layers of small stones with a surface of broken stone and grit.

MacAdam was not, as popularly thought,

the inventor of tarmacadam—he merely recommended it. In fact, before tar came into popular use, oil was spread on roads in a bid to reduce the dust clouds. In countries with moist climates, however, this method did not have permanent results. Consequently, in 1907, following successful trials, tar and other bituminous preparations were widely adopted.

Until then roads—especially in Britain— were almost as great an annoyance to motorists as the legislators. Ironically, it was because roads were so rough that the pneumatic tyre came into vogue—to improve the harsh ride from the rigid cart springs. Not surprisingly, the bad roads caused frequent punctures, which, in the early days, had to be repaired on the spot.

Getting started

When the car was in its infancy, its disadvantages were legion. The settings of the mixture and throttle controls literally depended on the weather. The carburettor had to be filled with petrol, and the engine started by cranking. Once it had fired, the

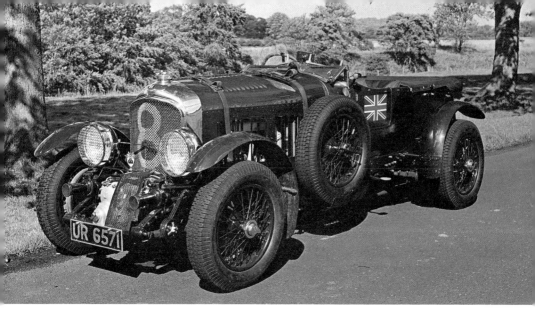

driver had to advance the ignition and, when on the move, watch the drip-feed lubrication very carefully. Blacksmiths were the early equivalent of the garage mechanic, but the wise motorist carried as many spares as he could, including a bucket for water and stout pieces of timber in case he needed to prise his car out of soft mud.

▲ The 4½-litre racing Bentley of 1929.

Beginnings of an industry

The situation could only improve—and it did. As industrialization brought greater prosperity, the numbers of the middle class increased and car ownership rose dramatically—particularly when Henry Ford conceived the assembly line. Indeed, his Model T—subsequently built in several countries—continued in manufacture for 19 years, during which time 15 million were made (a production record that has only recently been broken).

The top end of the market flourished, too. With famous names such as Rolls Royce, Mercedes, Bugatti and Hispano-Suiza came an era of romance and elegance that has never been surpassed.

▼ The pre-war age of elegance is epitomized by this poster for an MG. The venue is the Ascot races.

A somewhat fanciful creation for the fashionable motorist. More common headgear for women was a flat hat with a voluminous veil which covered the whole of the wearer's head and was fastened at the neck. A long dust-coat completed the outfit.

▼ Because pumps were manually operated, filling up was laborious, but it was an improvement on carrying the fuel in cans.

Without doubt, the peak of perfection was reached with the creation of the Phantom III Rolls, the Bugatti Royale and, perhaps, the most fabulous car ever made— the Hispano-Suiza Type 68 V12.

Introduced in 1931, the 9424cc Type 68 was capable of more than 100 mph. Comparatively few were made—and with an asking price in those days of £4000 it was perhaps hardly surprising. The survivors are the most sought-after and prized post-vintage collectors' pieces in existence.

The increasing popularity of the motor car is shown by the fact that, in Britain alone, ownership rose by 8000 a year between 1910 and 1914, by 70,000 a year between 1918 and 1923, and by 100,000 a year from 1924 until 1939.

Small wonder. The cost of motoring actually became cheaper as the years passed. The Model T was the most startling example. Owing to Ford's mass-production techniques, its selling price dropped from $500 in 1916 to $400, a price which remained steady until 1927. As for petrol, in Britain, for example, it cost just under 4p a gallon at the turn of the century, rising to about 9p in 1913. Then the effects of

▲ Rolls-Royce has always been synonymous with perfection in motor cars. This Silver Ghost in 1932 graces the entrance of a hotel at Le Touquet.

World War I pushed it up to 23p, but not for long. By 1928 it was down to 6p and, in the next eleven years, it increased by only $3\frac{1}{2}$p. Its quality improved out of all recognition, too.

It had to. Even in 1914 it was appreciated that, unless the volatility of fuel could be increased, it would be impossible to make engine power any greater. This became especially apparent when designers attempted to solve the problem by boosting combustion pressure.

This they tried to do simply by raising the compression ratio, and physically strengthening components to withstand the added stress and strain. But when manufacturers did just this, engine knock became so bad that the full power potential could not be realized.

Finally, research by British chemist Sir Harry Ricardo among others discovered that this could be prevented by mixing the petrol with certain additives such as lead.

With that, a brand-new branch of science was opened up, and work continues to this day. As a result, octane ratings have risen from 40 to 100, and engine performances increased accordingly—much to the concern of environmentalists worried about the effects of lead pollution on crops and the atmosphere.

The garage boom

At first petrol was sold mainly at chemists' shops because so many of the early cars were owned by doctors, who were able to

▼ The incredible Ford Model T which brought motoring to the masses and which is still in common use in some countries.

31

fill up their petrol tanks at the same time as collecting their patients' prescriptions. But by 1900 ironmongers, post offices and a few of the first garages had also begun to dispense it in two-gallon cans. The first actual filling station with pumps was built at Aldermaston, Berkshire, in 1920 by the Automobile Association. The AA had been founded 15 years previously, mainly to warn members of police speed traps.

The "Beetle"

In the same way that the Model T was the phenomenon of the age from 1908 to 1927, so the Volkswagen Beetle has eclipsed the sales of all rivals since the late '30s. Recently in fact it actually outsold Ford's 'Tin Lizzie', and has remained in production twice as long. Remarkably, apart from acquiring additional features of the kind embodied in most post-war models, it has hardly changed at all.

German manufacturers, whom Hitler had expected to collaborate on the building of the 'people's car', did not welcome the prospect of the Beetle, mainly because it was small. So in 1938 the Nazis constructed both a new factory and the town of Wolfsburg to mass-produce the 'Strength Through Joy Car' (as they called it).

Post war

As a war-ravaged Europe began to clear the rubble and rebuild, it was not surprising that, after years of oppression and austerity, people were yearning for improved living standards and an end to the shortages.

Industry and trading gradually recovered, and once more the means of acquiring life's luxuries became available. It was not long before the car became the most coveted of them all.

In Britain, the total number of motor vehicles in use doubled between 1953 and 1961, and had doubled again by 1971. In fact, ownership leapt from $2\frac{3}{4}$ million to $12\frac{1}{2}$ million over the 18-year period.

But times have changed, for Britain and for Europe. The late '60s proved the spring-board for a world-wide challenge by the Japanese. Their success was founded on the realization that just because something is new, it does not mean that it is the best. So while other manufacturers have wooed customers with increasingly sophisticated gadgetry—which, like so many new things, may suffer minor teething troubles—the Japanese have fitted well-tried, proven

▼ It is predicted that the United Kingdom will be self-sufficient in oil by 1980 — the date when, if all goes to plan, North Sea oil production should exceed Britain's requirements of two million barrels a day.

▲ More and more commuters are turning to two-wheel transport as congested roads and limited parking facilities make city car driving nerve shattering.

systems that may not be as sophisticated but can be infinitely more reliable.

The '60s will also be remembered as the decade when the world's manufacturers made their models safer. The new emphasis on safety followed the campaigns of the American consumer crusader, Ralph Nader, whose shock revelations triggered a wave of legislation in the United States and have had similar effect in other countries.

The '70s

The '70s will go down as the era when a global trade recession led to decreased individual wealth and soaring inflation—problems that have been compounded by the steep rises in fuel prices and the growing threat of total exhaustion of the earth's oil resources. Recent oil discoveries in the North Sea will help Britain's economy but will not make a significant contribution to world needs.

In this context of rising prices and shrinking prosperity, it is hardly surprising that more and more people are giving up motoring. For almost unbelievably, in the period between 1972 and 1976, the cost of running an average family saloon shot up by 46 per cent. Particularly noticeable has been the increase in the sales of mopeds—which are far cheaper to run than cars—and bicycles.

It is perhaps scarcely any wonder that a recent survey showed that already 8 per cent of motorists felt the time had come to start considering whether to stop driving altogether.

More than 60 per cent also declared that they were driving more slowly in a bid to reduce their fuel bill. Indeed nearly three-quarters of the owners questioned said that they were economizing in some way. Just over a tenth, for example, claimed that they were making economies in the home in order to keep their cars running—cutting back on electricity, food and clothing, and putting off buying a colour TV. Some, too, had given up smoking. But generally it is the car itself on which economies are being made. And for many, that simply means driving less.

Looking ahead

Such are the demands of the modern world that we will need as much oil in the next ten years as we have used in the last 100. Small wonder then that we are being told that our planet's natural oil resources will run out by the end of the century, that nations totally dependent on oil production are continually increasing the cost per barrel to safeguard their future, and that oil companies are spending millions searching for new oilfields. Yet, remarkably, man has tapped only a fraction of the oil under the Earth's surface.

So why is there an acute shortage? Simply because economical extraction of oil relies on nature to force it up to the surface; once this natural pressure is spent, the oil stops flowing. So until a cheap man-made alternative can be found, up to two thirds of the world's known oil deposits will remain underground.

Just as galling is the fact that, for the want of an inexpensive processing method, vast quantities of oil-bearing shale and tar sands which could more than double the world's known oil reserves, are largely unexploited. Coal, too, of which the world has plenty, can be turned into synthetic crude oil—but, on current technology, the cost of conversion is again prohibitively high.

The price of oil can only continue to rise and, because we rely on the stuff for practically everything, that will inevitably mean never-ending price increases all round. Especially in motoring.

For some while, the increases in a car's running costs have run slightly above the general cost of living index spiral; and by the look of things, the situation will worsen.

It wasn't so long ago that a house and its maintenance was the biggest item on the income earner's budget. But when looked at in the light of monthly loan repayments, insurance premiums, servicing, spare parts and repair bills, and all the other regular outgoings, it's scarcely surprising that the family car is running the family home an increasingly closer second in terms of expenditure.

Finding a new fuel

Will motoring ever be as cheap again as in the post-war car boom? Only when prac-

▼ The dazzling instrumentation of a new Ferrari.

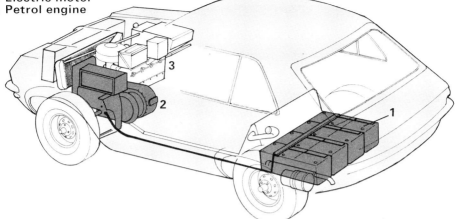

1. Batteries
2. Electric motor
3. Petrol engine

▲ Providing that the price is right, cars fitted with a petrol-driven engine and an auxiliary electric motor could well prove a part-solution to the oil crisis. In years to come, it's hoped that ways will be devised to enable the batteries to be revitalized by the petrol engine. Charging and storing continue to be the big problems.

tical alternative means of propulsion have been discovered and, after initial development, can the price be successfully lowered —like the price of the car was lowered by mass-production after 1908.

The most likely alternatives? According to the experts: electricity, hydrogen and solar power...

Electric power

When it is considered that in 1891 an electric car ran for 13 hours at a shade under 15 mph and that the performance of one recent experimental model, the Ford Comuta, was a range of 40 miles at 25 mph, it can be readily appreciated that electric vehicle technology has scarcely advanced in leaps and bounds.

Clearly there's much to be done if electricity is to become a feasible alternative to petrol—that is, if the electric car is ever to progress from being merely a local runabout. Indeed, just as in the early days of the internal combustion engine, its only attraction at present is its novelty value. And as in the old days, too, it is an expensive novelty—one short-lived British venture of late, the Enfield, retailed for nearly £3000.

The stumbling block is storing sufficient electricity to achieve the range attained by petrol cars in between battery recharging or exchange replacement. Currently, much research is being devoted to these problems.

The first practical answer, now being investigated by a British university, could well be a combined petrol-electric power unit. The theory is that once the electricity is exhausted, the driver would run for a while with a conventional petrol engine which, in addition to driving the vehicle, would quickly recharge the batteries.

Whether a car with two engines could ever be financially viable only time will tell. But one thing is for sure; the advantages of even partial electric drive are attractive— no gears, quietness and simplicity of operation, minimum pollution of the atmosphere and reduced running costs.

1. **Tank containing liquid hydrogen**
2. **Monitor and control system**
3. **Hydrogen supply**
4. **Regulator**

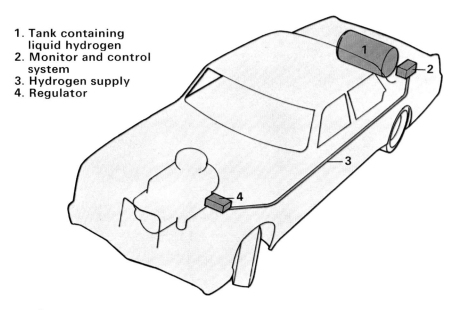

Hydrogen power

Three main benefits are derived from harnessing hydrogen—it is cheaper than petrol, its exhaust is virtually pollution-free, and conventional petrol engines can be converted to run on it.

The other attraction is that the gas is extracted from water. And water, unlike crude oil, is hardly likely to run out.

The drawbacks have been in finding a safe method of storing this volatile fuel, and in producing the gas in vast quantities.

One American company has made a significant step forward by developing both a liquid and a powder hydrogen system, using modified carburation and a specially packaged fuel supply.

In the "powder" system, the hydrogen is stored in dry iron-titanium powders in a special tank. In the "liquid" model, liquid hydrogen is stored in a thermos-like container at $-423°F$. The powder concept is the most favoured development because storage is simpler. As an interim measure, however, the emphasis is likely to be placed on a steam reforming process which generates hydrogen from petrol.

By carrying out tests on the Chevrolet, the firm has estimated that it is almost 30 per cent cheaper to run a car on hydrogen than it is to run a car on petrol. Hydrogen will certainly become an even better proposition as the price of crude oil continues to rise.

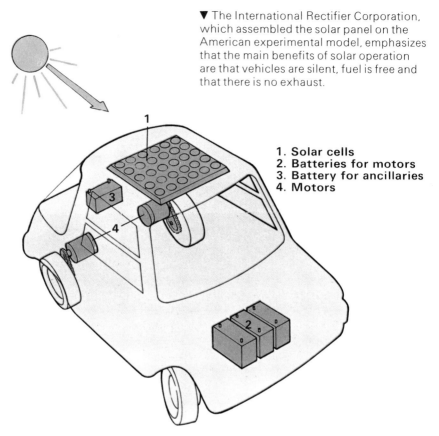

▼ The International Rectifier Corporation, which assembled the solar panel on the American experimental model, emphasizes that the main benefits of solar operation are that vehicles are silent, fuel is free and that there is no exhaust.

1. Solar cells
2. Batteries for motors
3. Battery for ancillaries
4. Motors

Solar power

Buying a car with a sunshine roof is likely to take on a whole new meaning in the future. Its purpose would not be to provide extra ventilation for passengers, instead, it would be a special device designed to actually power the vehicle.

The Americans proved it was possible back in 1960 by installing a panel of solar cells on top of an electric car. The cells, made of wafers of silicon crystal treated with a boron compound, converted sunlight into about 100 watts of power at 115 volts.

Another application being looked into is the conversion of solar energy into heat which would herald the return of the steam car.

Once again, the major obstacle is storage to keep the car going in cloudy weather and at night. On an optimistic note, the cost of solar units is expected to plunge by 90 per cent in the next ten years.

In a British experiment, an electric car has been fitted with a solar panel made by the Lucas company. However, its purpose is not to produce electricity for the engine, but for the lighting and ancillary systems. The aim is to conserve maximum power from the traction batteries for the drive, thus eliminating the tendency for lights to dim as battery power decreases. This could quite possibly be the first step to something much more exciting.

What you need

Because of their increasing sophistication and complicated gadgetry, most cars in current production offer little scope for the well-meaning but inexperienced do-it-yourself enthusiast to undertake many minor adjustments, let alone major repairs. But prevention is better than cure and you will find that getting into the habit of making regular, simple checks and carrying out basic maintenance at the recommended intervals will help to keep unwelcome garage bills at bay.

Motoring has become so expensive that few owners have a sufficient cash reserve to take care of running repairs and replacements and, most important of all, maintenance. All of which explains the poor mechanical state of many cars on the road.

Of the $2\frac{1}{2}$ million breakdowns attended each year by the world's largest motoring organization, the British Automobile Association, more than 42 per cent are attributable to maintenance neglect. Indeed the AA expects the 50 per cent barrier to be broken very soon.

The inescapable fact is that today, more than ever before, basic car care is vital. For it could well mean the difference between running a car and getting rid of it because of the expense of having it repaired regularly — an expense that would almost certainly be avoided if the vehicle was looked after properly. There can be no doubt that if owners cared for a car as they do in the first month or two after purchase, it would not only be less trouble-prone, it would last longer.

The intention of this book is not to waste your time by encouraging you to undertake tasks beyond your capability. The purpose of the activities in this section — mostly simple servicing and regular checking — is to help you to nip major trouble in the bud. You may well have to pay to have some of the minor problems sorted out, but it will only cost you a fraction of what you might have to pay if the little things are allowed to go on unobserved until they turn into big things.

Shopping around
Another sensible economy measure is to shop around for the bits and pieces you'll want to keep your car in trim before you need them — by looking for the true bargains at discount stores and at sales time. If you're caught out on the road, the chances are you will have to find the full recommended price . . . as well as pay expensive charges for a garage to rescue you.

Most items you would be wise to have to hand are listed in the next column and illustrated opposite. One useful tip: buy oil in bulk (5 gallon drums) — it's cheaper.

▶ **Some useful equipment**
1 Top and bottom radiator and heater hoses.
2 Car ramps.
3 Chamois leather.
4 Battery fluid.
5 Methylated spirits (an alternative to windscreen wiper fluid).
6 Hydraulic fluid.
7 Jack handle.
8 Jack.
9 Engine oil (and other handbook-recommended oils).
10 Foot pump.
11 Screwdrivers (large and small for slotted screws and Philips).
12 Wheel brace.
13 Grease gun.
14 Damp start spray.
15 Set of spanners. (Consult handbook for appropriate sizes.)
16 Grease. (Check handbook for recommended type).
17 Tyre valves.
18 Tyre pressure gauge.
19 Spare bulbs.
20 Electrical screwdriver.
21 Touch-up paint.
22 Paint primer.
23 Emergency fanbelt.
24 Fuses.
25 Sparking plug.
26 Pliers.
27 Sparking plug spanner.

Periodic checks

You're about to use the car, so what do you do? Almost certainly jump in, start up . . . and away. The fact is that motorists rarely bother to look round their vehicle before setting off. And it's not as if basic checks take very long – just a few minutes, that's all. But they could prove the most vital moments of your life: they could spell the difference between arriving at your destination safely and becoming an accident statistic.

It's ironic that motorists would never dream of boarding a plane unless they were sure it had been thoroughly checked. Yet the same drivers will think nothing of hopping into a car and starting off without giving it as much as a glance.

Perhaps more would if they saw the conclusions of a five-year study by a transport and road research laboratory. Vehicle defects, the report shows, are a contributory cause of one in 12 accidents, and most of the faults found could have been averted if only owners had carried out basic checks before setting off.

Before you start

The illustration opposite pinpoints the items you should inspect each time you use the car:

1. Switch on your parking lights and walk round the car to ensure that the side, tail, and rear number plate lamps work. Then put on the dipped and main beam headlamps to make sure they function properly (a bulb failure could lull an oncoming motorist into mistaking you for a motorcyclist with potentially disastrous results). Also confirm that the direction indicators, hazard warning lights and brake lamps are operating. And if any lights have a film of traffic grime, clean it off.

2. Keep inside and outside windscreen surfaces clean. In very cold weather, clear all windows and exterior mirror reflectors of frost with a de-icing aerosol.

3. Look for evidence of oil, petrol, hydraulic fluid and water leaks on ground over which your car has been standing (see also p. 53).

4. Check the level of the brake hydraulic fluid reservoir. This is most important – it will indicate any fluid loss at a glance. If the level has fallen below the minimum line, a system failure could be imminent. In Britain alone, 2500 accidents a year are caused by hydraulic brake malfunction, which underlines the need for regular reservoir inspection. If the level is under the minimum mark, then it is imperative that the car is not driven until the fault is put right and the system topped up and bled. If, on the other hand, the level is between the maximum and minimum markers, top up with new fluid (never use old), and pump the pedal a few times. Then recheck the level.

5. Some cars have a separate clutch reservoir. The guidance under 4 applies.

6. Making sure the car is on flat ground, withdraw the oil sump dipstick, wipe clean, and replace. Remove it again and, if the oil level is shown to be below the maximum marker, top up with fresh oil of the correct grade. If frequent topping-up is necessary, have the system investigated. Regular checking is important: oil starvation could seriously damage the engine.

7. Check the coolant level in the radiator or equalizing tank, and top up if necessary. If constant topping-up is needed, have the system examined: a serious loss could cause severe engine damage.

8. Look at each tyre and inspect closely for cuts, abrasions, bulges and tread damage; don't forget to feel round the inside walls. If in doubt about anything, have it checked by an expert. See pages 42 and 52 for further guidance.

9. Always keep the windscreen washer reservoir topped up.

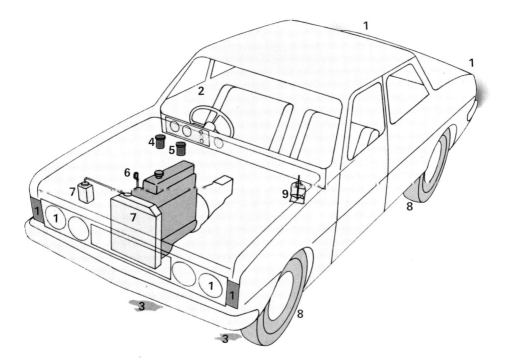

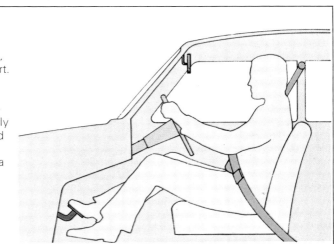

Driving position
Correct driving position is vital for proper control and, to avoid fatigue, for comfort. With the lever provided, adjust the seat until your knees and elbows are half-bent. Your feet should easily depress the foot pedals and your hands comfortably hold the steering wheel in a 'ten-to-two' position. Finally, make sure that the seat is locked and your driving mirror is correctly adjusted.

The battery

Once a week (more regularly in hot weather), remove the protective caps or strip from the filler holes (1) in the top of the battery and inspect the electrolyte level (2) in each cell. It should be about 5 mm ($\frac{1}{4}$ in) above the plates. Pour in distilled or deionised water as necessary, but be careful not to overfill otherwise you could weaken the electrolyte. Finally replace the caps or strip and mop up any spillage. Occasionally remove the battery leads; then clean the terminal posts (3, 4) and connections, rub with a fine emery cloth, and smear with petroleum jelly before refitting. Also make sure that the connection to the car body of the braided earth lead (5) is clean.

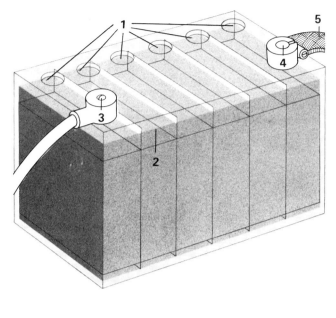

The tyres

Check tyre pressures once a week to the manufacturer's specifications – don't forget the spare. But don't rely too much on the accuracy of a gauge on a garage forecourt. Instead measure the amount of air with a reliable pocket gauge, obtainable from most accessory shops. If the pressure in any of the tyres has dropped more than 3 pounds per square inch at the next check, have the tyre examined by an expert. The importance of correct tyre inflation cannot be stressed too highly. Incorrect pressures can mar roadholding and stability and lead to premature, costly replacement.

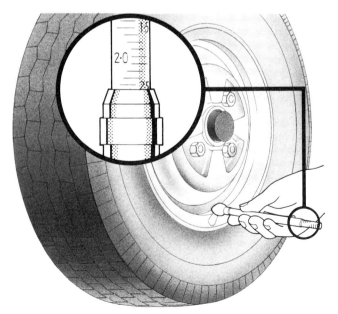

1. Tread depth

Make a point, too, of occasionally inspecting the tread depth of each tyre with a tread depth gauge. Check each groove and, if the depth is less than 2mm, get the tyre replaced. If replacement is necessary, bear in mind that new tyres need to be run in and do not exceed 50mph for the first 100 miles. You should have your tyres checked by an expert every three months or 3000 miles.

While on the subject of wheels, ensure at least once a month that the wheel nuts are tight. A useful tip; remove the nuts altogether and lightly coat the threads of the wheel studs with graphite grease. Should you ever be caught out with a puncture, the business of taking off a wheel will be made that much easier.

When replacing the nuts. remember that the rounded ends go on first.

2. Sparking plugs

These should be serviced by a garage every 5000 miles and replaced at 10,000 miles so keep a written log of your mileage. When plugs are changed, make sure that the gap between the centre and earth electrodes is set to the manufacturer's recommendation. Also jot down the mileage at which the contact breaker points are renewed — they should be checked by an expert every 5000 miles.

3. Wiper blades

As soon as the windscreen wiper blades become worn — that is, when they lose their spring and sharp wiping edge 'change them. And always buy the best.

4. Fanbelt

Play in the fanbelt should never exceed 20mm ($\frac{3}{4}$in); a check for tension and wear should be made at least once every four weeks, with adjustment or replacement as necessary.

5. Hoses

Also once a month, examine the condition of the top and bottom coolant hoses, and replace if there is evidence of cracking or undue chafing particularly around the clips. For good measure, also inspect the heater, fuel, brake and, if fitted, vacuum servo hoses.

6. Seatbelts

These are another monthly check. See that the mounting bolts are tight, the anchor points pivot, and the webbing is neither frayed nor worn.

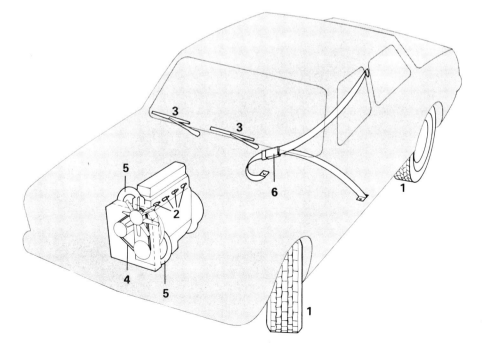

Cleaning and rust treatment

A brand new car gets a shampoo and bath perhaps once a week. But when enthusiasm wanes, it only gets a wash and brush up when the owner feels like it, which means there are progressively longer intervals between each session. If only we went on as we started! The fact is that a car should be washed once a week. And if it was, it would last considerably longer, as well as improve its resale price potential.

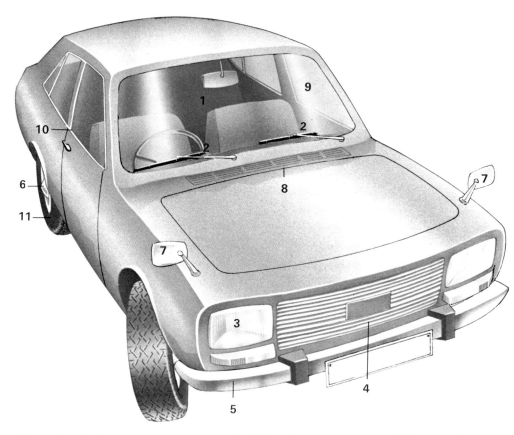

It's a fact that most cars could be better made. But the truth, all too often, is that a car's worst enemy is not so much age deterioration but owner neglect. In other words, there's no reason why your model even a dozen years from now shouldn't look every bit as smart as it did the day you drove it out of the showroom. that is, providing you look after it.

The first essential is to avoid automatic car washes which can harm the finish. Do the job by hand with a hose and special brush attachment, not a cloth or sponge which may only succeed in grinding minute grit particles into the paintwork.

Shampooing and rinsing
This should be done out of direct sunlight, and in this order: roof, bonnet, boot lid, rear, nearside, front, offside, and wheels. Shampooing is

best done with tepid water; rinsing with cold. (Dull paintwork, if caused by traffic haze, can be removed by adding a little paraffin to the water; tar spots should be erased with white spirit then rinsed with water.) After rinsing, dry with a chamois leather, but make sure that it is clean and free of grit.

The rest of the car

This can best be tackled in the following way.

1. The windscreen (and rear window): never treat with shampoo, polish or a proprietary window cleaner. Wash thoroughly with water and dry with a separate chamois leather reserved exclusively for the purpose. Occasionally treat the windscreen rubber sealant with boot polish.

2. Wiper blades: never use grease or polish. Clean with a cloth soaked in undiluted windscreen washer additive or household ammonia.

3. Lamp glass should be kept clean at all times.

▲ Use a hose with a special soft brush attachment. Some types are available with a shampooing unit in the brush handle.

▲ The peril of using an automatic car wash or cleaning with a cloth is that it can produce thousands of minute scratches in the paintwork.

Stubborn marks should be removed with a proprietary cleaner. Also get rid of all embedded dirt round lamp surrounds, and dry thoroughly.

4. Radiator grille: thoroughly shampoo and rinse both sides of all decorative strips with the hose brush attachment, temporarily removing badges and auxiliary lamps if they're in the way.

5. Metal bumpers (front and rear) should be taken off now and again, and the hidden side cleaned then treated with silicon wax polish which should not be buffed. Similarly treat the bodywork normally concealed by the bumpers.

6. Wheel trim: shampoo and wash with the hose brush. Stubborn marks should be treated with a stiff brush and paraffin, and rinsed off with water. Both hub caps and trim should be taken off occasionally to clean the hidden side. Like

the bumper interiors, also treat with wax polish and, again, don't buff off. Similarly treat the wheel sections normally concealed by the hub caps and trim.

7. Exterior mirrors: do not shampoo or polish the glass. Wash thoroughly with water, and dry with a chamois leather.

8. Windscreen washer nozzles can be blocked by polish and dirt. Pierce with a length of strong, thin gauge wire, taking care not to alter the nozzle settings.

9. Side windows can be treated with a proprietary cleaner if they are very dirty. Don't forget to remove dirt from the window guides. Also occasionally apply boot polish to the rubber window seals.

10. Brightwork (chrome fittings) should be shampooed and rinsed the same way as paintwork. Only resort to chrome polish when marked or tarnished. Never use metal polish.

11. Tyre walls: wash thoroughly and, after drying, paint the walls with tyre black if necessary. Never use petrol to clean tyres or other rubber parts.

Final advice: wax polish the bodywork twice a year — at the beginning and end of winter. But ensure that car polish is used. (Other polishes can dull paintwork.) Never apply polish until a car is at least two months old; also allow two months after a respray. Use proprietary anti-haze preparations sparingly and carefully — they are mildly abrasive.

CLEANING INSIDE

1. Interior mirror: clean with a solution of warm water and methylated spirit (add just a few drops of meths until the water begins to cloud), rinse, then dry with a chamois leather.

2. Upholstery: neglect can lead to permanent discolouration of the covering fabric and dirty seats can soil light-coloured clothes. Use the appropriate proprietary cleaner for the material — never detergent or any preparation containing bleach. For leather and plastic surfaces lightly brush or vacuum then, with a cloth or sponge, wash with the recommended cleansing agent which should be diluted with warm water. Do not soak and after rinsing, dry with a soft cloth. Remove stubborn marks with undiluted cleanser, then rinse and dry. Cloth fabrics should be lightly brushed or vacuumed, then wiped with a soft cloth that has been dipped in the recommended cleaning fluid. Rinse (taking care not to soak the fabric), and dry.

3. Seats: (front): clean and lightly lubricate the adjustment mechanism, and occasionally lightly grease the runners. Rear: take out the cushion section and vacuum any dirt that may have collected on the floor section underneath.

4. Windows and panels: shampoo, rinse and leather any paintwork (the top, bottom and inside edges of the door, and the door frames, too). For treatment of panelling trim, follow upholstery cleaning advice, but it is even more imperative that you do not use too much water, otherwise you could distort the board to which, in many cases, the panel fabric is attached. The same applies to the front and rear parcel shelves; also be sparing with the water when cleaning the trim around the dashboard instruments. Clean all interior window surfaces the same way as

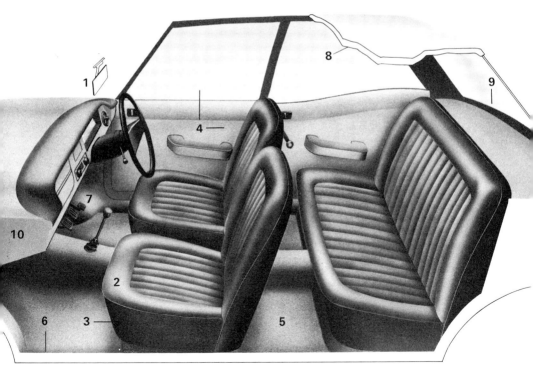

the mirror.

5. Floor covering: one of the most vital jobs on the interior cleaning programme (for long life) is removing the carpet or rubber matting, a job which is unfortunately fiddly on many models: in most cases, retaining trim has to be removed first. Why manufacturers cannot return to the good old days of simple stud fastening right the way round is beyond comprehension, particularly when regular examination of the floorpan is advisable. Rubber matting, once removed, is easily brushed and washed clean. Carpets, however, call for more care. They should be vacuumed frequently to get rid of harmful grit, and treated occasionally with a proprietary carpet cleaner.

6. Floorpan: after brushing or vacuuming any dirt, dust and grit, inspect the floorpan for moisture, paint chipping and corrosion. Any one of these can trigger unwelcome rust. Paint damage and rust spots are dealt with on page 51. Moisture has three possible causes; leaks (in which case suspect a hole or open weld seam, or a perished or damaged door or window weather strip); wet footwear (dampness from which may have soaked through the carpet); and 'sweating' through condensation (rubber and some man-made fibres do not allow the floor to 'breathe'). The floor, the carpet or matting, and any underlay

should be thoroughly dried before the covering is re-laid. Don't forget to clean under the front seats. When refitting carpet or matting, ensure that it fits properly around the foot pedals, and is not torn. If it should ruck up, or the driver gets a foot caught up in the tear, it could have disastrous consequences.

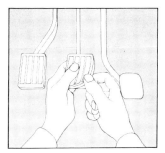

▲ Remove and inspect pedal rubbers.

7. The pedals: remove, and wash and dry the rubber covers. Replace if worn or split — they could cause your foot to slip off.

8. Roof lining (and sun visor fabric): plastic material should be wiped lightly with a moist cloth dipped in a diluted solution of a preparation made specially for the task. Do not rub stubborn marks — instead use undiluted cleansing fluid. Cloth linings should first be gently brushed or vacuumed, then given a light rub-over with a soft cloth that has been dipped in the recommended cleansing fluid. Hard rubbing could tear the material.

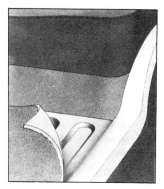

▲ Remove carpets to inspect and clean floorpan.

9. The boot: clean and vacuum regularly, and check for leaks (suspect perished weather strip, open weld seams or perished or ill-fitting drainhole bungs). To treat paint damage or rust, refer to page 51. Don't forget the underside of the boot lid.

10. The engine compartment: frequent cleaning of paintwork, the top of the engine and the various components will make regular attentions to the engine easier and kinder to the hands. Don't forget the underside of the bonnet. Cleaning the nooks and crannies will also help to prevent rust.

Other attentions: if damaged, split or worn, replace the protective rubber gaiters around the gear lever and the handbrake. Also check that ventilation and hot air ducts, and audio equipment speaker grilles are free of obstructions and dust.

Cleaning underneath

This is only a twice-a-year job to be done at the beginning and end of winter, yet few motorists ever bother, which explains why many cars rapidly deteriorate and, worse, become unsafe.

Unless the underneath is cleaned periodically mud, thrown up by the road-wheels, will cling and cake to structural box sections, on which the car depends for its strength and rigidity. The mud poultices, activated by moisture, contain substances that are very harmful to metal.

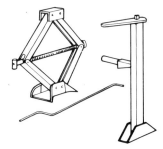

▶ Jacking points may be found at any of these locations, so check your handbook.

Raising the car

The first essential, unless you have access to a pit or a hoist, is to give yourself room to move. Three ways are shown in the panel below, and two of them involve the use of jacks. The diagram, also on this page, illustrates the points where a jack may be placed without damaging a car.

The side locations are jacking points normally supplied specifically for the purpose by manufacturers (but refer to the handbook to determine the precise positions on your model). The only other locations strong enough to take the strain are, as depicted, on the suspension, but these are only suitable for the scissors (1) and other all-

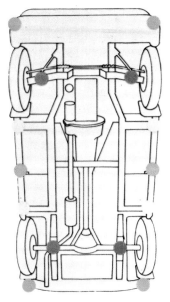

purpose jacks. The other type of jack (2), supplied with some cars, can only be used in the special side sockets provided.

Underside rust

This problem is accentuated

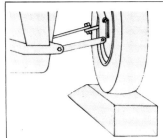

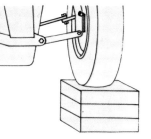

When working underneath

Drive one pair of wheels onto ramps built for the purpose, apply hand-brake and chock the other wheels. NB.— Wheels cannot be taken off.

Only use a jack on firm, level ground. Apply hand-brake and chock. After raising the car, place stout wooden blocks under the wheels or jacking points.

After jacking the car, place axle stands under jacking points. Then, by lowering the jack, guide the car gently onto the supports so the weight is taken as shown.

by highly corrosive salt from winter roads, and stone and grit bombardment at all times.

Never be lulled into thinking that the underneath can take care of itself, even if anti-corrosive treatment extends to box section interiors. Welded seams frequently leave unprotected areas to the mercy of the elements and, in any case, unless coverage of the compound in the box sections is total (which it usually isn't), corrosion attack can be concentrated on the untreated areas with even more rapid and damaging results.

In addition, it's possible that some dry dust and other pollutants, picked up from the air and the road, can harm primers and other protective coatings which have been formulated principally to guard against rust.

Unfortunately that's something none of us can do anything about, though there are plenty of other precautions which can usefully be taken. The first priority is to wear old clothes, headgear and goggles (other points to watch are set out on page 70). The diagram on this page shows the likeliest places where mud will collect.

Points to attend to

1. The wheel arches: having jacked the car and taken steps to enable you to work underneath safely, take off each wheel in turn and dislodge as much mud as you can without touching the metal (give particular atten-

tion to the very top of the arches). Then remove the remainder with a tough nylon bristle brush.

2. The sills: Locate the ventilation holes and ensure that they are not blocked. This is important because the purpose of ventilation is to allow air to circulate and dry any moisture. If the holes are blocked, trapped moisture will cause corrosion. So clear any obstructions with a sharp piece of

wire. Then shampoo, rinse and dry with a leather any paintwork in the sill area. N.B. Similarly treat all door undersides.

3. Mudflaps: Mud frequently poultices in nooks and crannies around the mudflaps. Clean off with the nylon bristle brush.

When you have attended to these points, brush down the rest of the underside, and pressure hose the whole of the underneath.

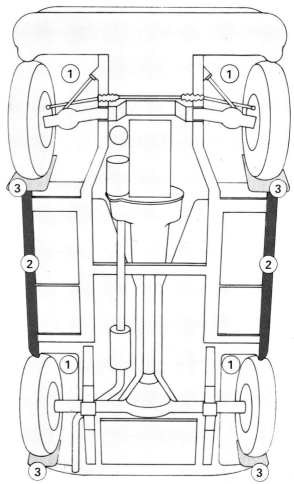

Rust prevention

Although most models to-day are given underbody and other protective treatments on the assembly line to help prevent corrosion, it is still most advisable to have a vehicle thoroughly rustproofed by a reputable firm specializing in the job. The comparatively low expense involved is worth it even if you have no intention of keeping the car very long, because it will almost certainly increase the value of the car when it comes up for resale.

It is often in the very areas that never occur to motorists, like door interiors and structural box sections, that rust is at its most destructive. Indeed, the bulk of the damage wrought by corrosion starts not from the outside but from the insides which, in many cases, are inaccessible.

The danger is that if vital load-bearing parts are allowed to corrode, the protection given to a car's occupants in a serious collision is very much reduced because the structure, instead of absorbing the shock of the impact and staying in one piece, collapses, sometimes with fatal results.

Treatment of interiors is definitely a job for the professional, for if the task is not done properly it is best not attempted at all. Incomplete coverage can actually accelerate corrosion.

As soon as a paint chip (a potential rust spot) or evidence of corrosion is noticed, no matter how small it may be, repair it at once, for rust spreads fast. And rust, remember, doesn't always give its presence away by its familiar reddish-brown colour. Be on the lookout too for paint-bubbling, which is a clear sign of rust underneath.

Regular examination of the whole car, inside and out, is essential. This includes the boot, the engine compartment and the underside, too. The diagram shows where rust is likeliest to strike on the underbody: the edges (including the jacking points and the sills) and the exhaust system which, in most cases, will only last around 18 months unless you're prepared to pay for a stainless steel type.

One final piece of advice: never store a wet car in a garage unless there is a through draught. Lack of

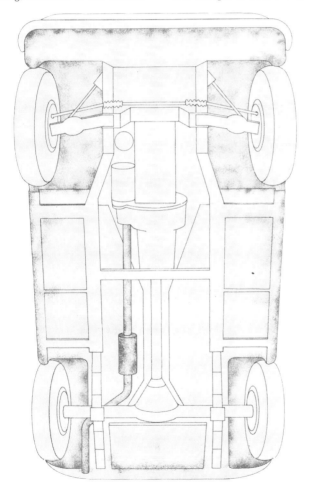

◀ Areas prone to rust.

ventilation will only accelerate corrosion.

Underbody rust
After cleaning the under-
body and allowing it to dry,
examine the whole area for
rust. The extreme edges are

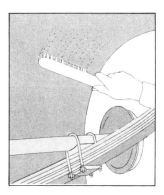

especially prone because,
when the compound is
sprayed on at the factory,
these areas are masked off
to prevent the sealant from
contaminating the body
paintwork. Later, a wax-
based inhibitor is brushed
on these untreated sections
by hand. But unfortunately,
the job is not always done as
thoroughly as it should be.
Even if it is, the inhibitor
dissolves in time through
weathering.

Be alert too for flaking,
bulging, cracking and miss-
ing sealing compound elsewhere.

Treat only when the
underbody and atmosphere
are dry. After removing damaged or flaking sealant, prise
away compound for about
an inch around the affected
area. Then, rusting or not,
clean to bare metal with a
wire brush.

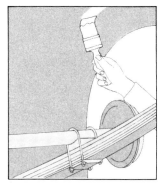

Replacement of primer and compound
The next step is to apply a
proprietary anti-rust solution. This may have to be
washed off immediately, for
some preparations prevent
the primer which follows
and the replacement underbody compound which goes
on after that from staying in
place. Follow the advice on
the canister to the letter.

Then brush on a coat of
primer. Once this is dry, you
can put on the underbody
protector. Using an old
brush, apply the compound
thickly, ensuring that you
work it into any crevices.
Use two coats for wheel
arches because these areas
take more punishment from
stones and the elements.

On no account apply
compound to the engine,
gearbox, clutch, steering,
brakes, suspension, transmission, any moving parts,
grease nipples or drainage
holes. Do not treat any part
of the exhaust, either, as the
heat could cause dangerous
fumes.

Also ensure that the com-
pound does not come in
contact with body paint-

work. If it should, remove it
immediately with paraffin.

Major corrosion repairs,
which could involve weld-
ing or filling, are best left to
a garage.

Retouching chips
Attend to minor paint chips
as soon as they are noticed
to prevent rust from setting
in.

Gently scrape away the
edges of the good paint and,
if you are satisfied that there
is no rust, apply lightly and
with a fine brush the right
shade and type of touch-up
paint for your car.

In the event of bubbles in

the paintwork (a sure sign
of rust underneath) and if
the bare metal uncovered
by a chip has rusted, scrape
away the good paint around
the damaged area until you
reach the limit of the rust's
spread. Then, with wet and
dry emery paper, clean down
to bright metal and feather
the edges of the good paint.

Thoroughly rinse with
water, dry, and apply a proprietary anti-rust solution.
Next, with a fine brush,
apply a coat of primer suitable for the touch-up finish.

Fault prevention

It's staggering that, despite the publicity given to recalls – when manufacturers, realizing that a faulty component may jeopardize safety, ask for cars to be returned to dealers to have the defect rectified – by no means do all owners respond. What chance then does the average motorist have of recognizing the symptoms of other troubles which could result in an accident? How likely is it that he will have to pay out far more than is necessary by allowing a minor problem to become a major one? The following pages show you how to spot the trouble and put a stop to it before it happens.

What the tyres tell you

Let's start with obvious warning signs you should be looking out for; obvious because, unlike most parts of a car, they are not hidden from sight.

The pattern of tyre tread wear, for instance, can tell you a great deal as the diagram shows. 1. Excessive wear of the centre of the tread indicates that the tyre is over-inflated. 2. Excessive wear of the outsides of the tread signifies under-inflation. 3. The penalty of a neglected cut in the tread and/or excessive speed: it has caused a chunk to be stripped off, rendering the tyre dangerous. 4. Uneven wear like this points to a wheel out of balance. 5. Excessive wear on one side means incorrect camber angle. 6. If the tread displays regular wear like this, suspect a defective suspension. 7. Flat spots localized in one area are indicative of the brakes locking or binding. 8. The track setting is incorrect if the tread on the outside edge is feathered or rippled.

Spot checks

Equally as obvious as tyre wear symptoms are the drips of tell-tale trouble that your car may leave on the road, driveway or garage floor after it has been standing for a while. Learn how to interpret these signs — the lesson could one day save your life. It could certainly save you money.

The diagram shows the marks you should be watching out for in the case of a conventional front-engine, rear-wheel drive car. From the location of these deposits you can work out the probable source of leaks.

So, after making a mental note of where the vehicle has been standing, move the car to another parking spot and study the space just vacated.

If you see a heavy deposit at 1 it means you are losing engine oil (this may not be too serious, but keep an eye on the oil sump level with the dipstick just the same. Run out of oil on a journey and you'll seize the engine). Leak 2 suggests oil loss from the gearbox so check the dipstick reading (refer to the car handbook for the gearbox dipstick location); if a serious leak is confirmed, have it investigated. Stain 3 suggests loss of hydraulic fluid from the brake master cylinder (don't use the car

until the fault has been remedied). Leak 4 implies that oil is escaping from the differential or rear axle (this too will need to be inspected to prevent potentially expensive damage). 5 is almost certainly a fuel tank drip (have this investigated without delay). 6 is a water coolant leak, so watch the level in the radiator tank. 7 like 3, could signify loss of hydraulic brake fluid — in this case from defective slave cylinders or flexible hoses. However, in the case of the rear wheels, it could mean that a rear axle oil seal has gone and oil contamination, note, could seriously affect the brakes.

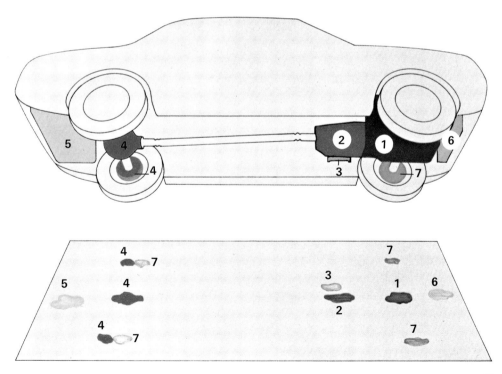

Brakes: Checking the system

First remove one of the wheels and refer to the car handbook for advice on how to slacken the brake shoe adjuster(s). Next, take off the drum by undoing the retaining screws then, if necessary, ease off by tapping the protruding rim, using a hammer and a block of wood. Once freed, clean the shiny inside surface of the drum with a rag dipped in methylated spirit, and check for scoring (see illustration). If the face isn't smooth, the drum will have to be replaced.

Now inspect the linings

and have them changed if they are loose, oil-fouled, or less than 2mm ($\frac{1}{16}$ in) thick above the shoe or rivet head, (see below).

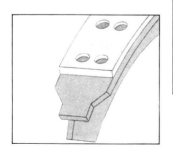

Slave cylinder

While it is accessible, examine the slave cylinder (1) and get the rubber dust covers replaced if perished. Also check for hydraulic fluid leaks. If you find any, you will almost certainly need to have the seals inside the cylinder renewed with-

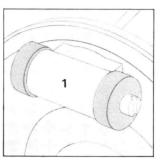

out delay. If the car has been standing for a while, another sign of leaking fluid is discolouration at the base of the drum on the outside (see below).

Finally reassemble, setting the brake shoe adjuster(s) to the handbook's recommendation. Repeat the operation on the opposite drum.

Discs and pads

Remove one of the wheels and check the thickness of the pads through the opening in the caliper casing (see illustration). The car handbook will tell you the recommended minimum. If one or both are near the limit, arrange to have the pads changed by an expert.

Also check both braking surfaces of the disc. If one shows signs of rust, have the brake examined by a garage — a caliper piston may have seized. Ensure too that the disc spins without resistance, and that both faces are smooth. If not, seek garage advice. And examine for oil and hydraulic brake fluid leaks at the base of the assembly (as shown).

Finally, replace the wheel,

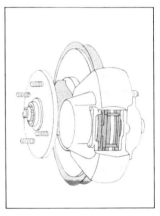

and repeat the operation on the other disc brake(s).

The hydraulic system

Make a point of inspecting the whole hydraulic system under the car occasionally. Your life could depend on it.

A typical system is shown right. It starts with the brake pedal (1), proceeds to the master cylinder (2) and continues to the roadwheels, for the most part in small diameter steel tubing. The final part of the journey to the backplate of each wheel, to which the slave cylinders are attached, is a flexible hose.

The three priorities are to examine for evidence of hydraulic fluid leaks, corrosion of the steel tubing, and wear and chafing of the flexible pipes.

First search for leaks: check all joints and T-pieces (3) and ensure that union nuts are tight. In addition, inspect the backplates of the roadwheels (4), including the bleed nipples.

Next, examine the steel tubing for signs of serious pitting and corrosion. Pay particular attention to the spots where the tubing is clipped to the underbody. If the securing clips are made of metal, rapid corrosion can take place in the area of contact. After this, check the flexible hoses for fatigue, damage and perishing.

Remedial work on any part of the braking system is best left to a garage.

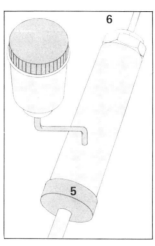

The master cylinder

Don't forget to inspect the exterior of the master cylinder for leaks. Check for evidence of hydraulic fluid loss on the rubber dust protector (5) and the union (6). Additionally, locate the inlet pipe leading from the reservoir and check all joints in this section.

Also inspect the rubber dust protector for damage and perishing, and have it renewed if necessary.

The handbrake

A typical layout, in which the handbrake is applied by the lever (7) simultaneously pulling two separate cables, is illustrated below, but there are several variations.

Because the moving parts on most systems are open to the weather, seizure is commonplace. Get someone to operate the lever to enable you to check the cable movement at 8 and 9. If seizure is apparent (also inspect swivels and pivots, if fitted), treat the affected area with penetrating oil. Also examine the cables for fraying, in which case they should be replaced. Ensure that adjustment is carried out to the manufacturer's recommendations.

If trouble persists, seek garage advice.

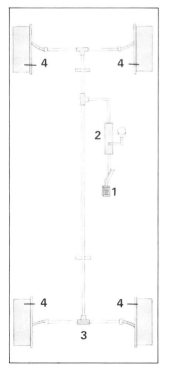

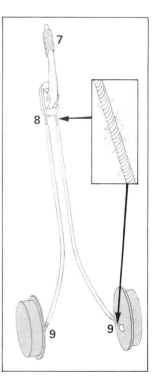

Transmission

Operation of a hydraulic clutch follows a similar pattern to the footbrake system. The pedal (1) causes a piston (2) to move in the master cylinder (3) which in turn compresses the hydraulic fluid in the pipeline (4). The pressure activates a piston in the slave cylinder (5), and this disengages the clutch.

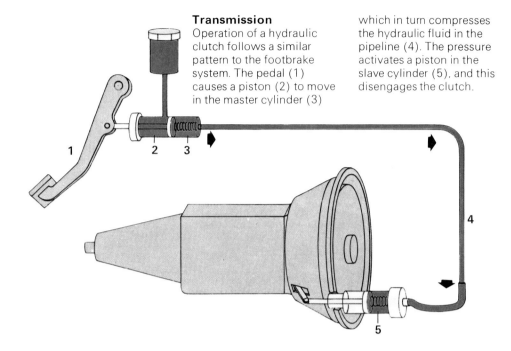

Hydraulic clutch

Unless you check the clutch system from time to time, you face the risk of one day being unable to get the car moving, simply because you won't be able to select gear.

In a hydraulic clutch lay-out (see above), inspect the complete system for leaks, particularly in the region of joints (and don't forget the inlet tube from the reservoir). Also examine the plastic tubing for chafing and damage, and the rubber dust protectors on the master and slave cylinders for signs of perishing and wear. Have them changed if necessary.

Look under the clutch housing too. If oil is present, seek garage advice; a gearbox or flywheel oil seal may have perished.

False economies

How much would you be prepared to spend over and above the price of a new car if you could be given an assurance that irksome bits and pieces, which have an early record of failure, would last a great deal longer?

The manufacturers insist that, because many owners rarely hold on to a car, purchased new, for longer than two or three years, it is unfair that they should pay over the odds for benefits that subsequent buyers will enjoy. But now there's growing evidence that more and more new car buyers are holding on to their vehicles longer before changing.

Britain's Automobile Association demonstrated early in 1977 that just a few pence more spent on components (that's all it would cost in volume production at the assembly stage) would make a marked difference to owner's running costs in the long run.

Says the AA: 'Most component failures would be phased out completely – or at the very least wouldn't happen so early in a car's life – if better quality methods were used'.

The trouble is that little things often lead to much bigger troubles with repair bills increasing

Engine mountings

Vibration from the engine gearbox unit is damped by three or four special mountings. These are simply rubber blocks (see below). Check the rubbers for sponginess, oil fouling and damage, and have them changed if necessary.

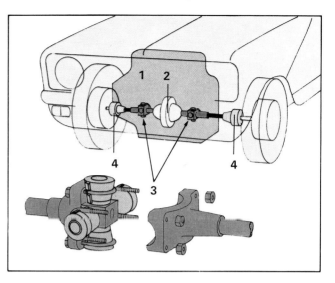

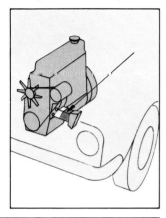

accordingly. If a water hose fails while a car is running, an expensive engine seizure could be triggered off. The life of hoses could be increased by up to three years if they were made of a better quality rubber. And the cost at the assembly stage would only be a few pence per unit. For about another £1.00 brake pipelines could be fitted that would be guaranteed corrosion-free for the life of a car. An extra few pence per unit would add two years to the life of rubber engine mountings and make protective rubber boots and gaiters last at least 35 per cent longer.

Front wheel drive

Transmission of power from the engine (1) to the road-wheels on front wheel drive cars is through the differential (2) and the drive shaft assembly which, on both the nearside and offside, includes a spider joint (3) or 'rubber doughnut' coupling, and constant velocity joint (4).

The first point to inspect is the lower part of the back of the spider joints or rubber doughnut couplings. If there is evidence of oil on either one, suspect a seal failure, a job for a garage.

Next, check the tightness of the bolts on these components and the rubber for oil contamination, cracking, wear or damage. Get the parts renewed if the rubber is perished.

Finally, examine the rubber protector boots around the constant velocity joints; if worn, have them changed.

The propshaft

On front engine, rear drive cars, check the propshaft universal joints (5 and 6) for wear by holding the universal joint flange with one hand and moving the propshaft from side to side with the other. Movement means the joint needs replacing.

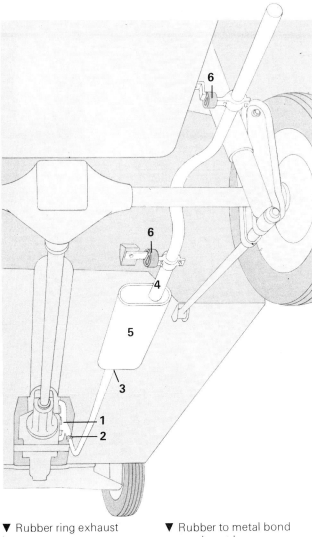

The exhaust system

The exhaust system, as millions of motorists annually find to their cost, is invariably one of the first components that has to be replaced. False economizing by manufacturers means that some exhaust units made of mild steel last only days beyond warranty period.

It is useless to discuss ways of repairing worn exhaust systems — the only permanent remedy is to buy a new one. Occasional checks still have to be carried out on the condition of the mountings which, if loose or broken, can damage or weaken the tubing and silencer box. Examination for leaks is also very important; a gas escape is highly dangerous. If it wafts into the passenger compartment, it can have fatal results.

First, get someone to rev the engine. While this is being done, inspect the manifold (1) at the point where it joins the cylinder head. If any gas can be seen or felt escaping or if the area is discoloured, have the gasket replaced.

Still keeping the engine running, inspect the rest of the system, not only at the joints (2, 3, 4) but along the whole route. Pass your hand as close as you can to the tubing and the silencer box (5) without touching them, feeling for leaks.

Also examine the condition of the rubber fixing rings, if fitted, and rubber mountings (6). If perished, replace them.

▼ Rubber ring exhaust hanger.

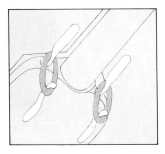

▼ Rubber to metal bond type exhaust hanger.

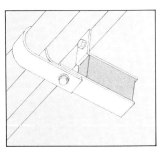

STEERING

Rack and pinion
▶ As the steering wheel is turned, a small pinion at the other end of the connecting shaft moves a toothed rack which causes the shafts attached to the wheels to swivel.

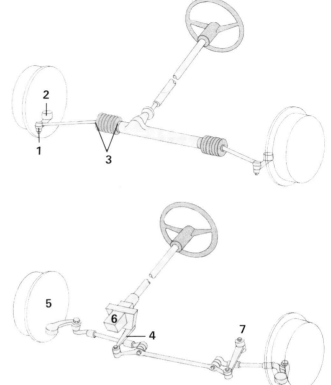

Steering box
▶ Like the rack and pinion method, the steering box system is a gear designed to minimize the effort needed on the steering wheel. At the other end of the connecting shaft a worm gear shifts a tapered peg. This is joined to a drop arm which moves the rest of the linkage.

Rack and pinion
Excessive wear in the swivel mechanisms (1) can affect steering efficiency to the point that it can become dangerous. To check, hold the steering arm running from 1 to 2 firmly and ask someone to turn the steering wheel. If there is movement in the ball joints (1) before the steering arm is activated, they are worn and will have to be replaced. Also check the ball joints (2) and, if fitted, the swivel mechanisms above them.

Ensure that the mounting brackets which secure the steering mechanism to the body or chassis are tight and that the rubber blocks sandwiched in them are in

good condition. If not, have them replaced.

Examine too the rubber in the coupling (if fitted) between the end of the steering column and the rack. If damaged or split, get it seen to.

Inspect the ends of the rubber protective boots (3). If there is any sign of oil, tighten the retaining clips. If the boots themselves are split or perished, have them renewed.

Steering box
Hold the drop arm (4) firmly and attempt to move it up and down and from side to side. If there is movement,

the bushes will have to be replaced. If your model has kingpins at (5), check their condition by firmly holding each front wheel in turn at the top and trying to move them backwards and forwards. If there is any play, have the kingpins and bushes renewed.

Also examine all ball joints, and repeat procedures outlined in the rack and pinion section. Inspect the tightness of the steering box (6) and idler box (immediately above the drop arm, 7).

N.B. Replacement of steering parts is a job for a garage.

▲ Modern suspension units are designed to withstand punishing treatment as this rally car is demonstrating.

Suspension: fault prevention

To many, the term 'suspension' simply means the car's springs, designed to make life more comfortable for the occupants. Obviously this is one of the functions of the suspension, but its more important role is safety: to improve steering and stability. Few drivers realize just how much punishment the roadwheels are subjected to. At any given second they will be going up and down, from side to side, or both. Not only that, but additional loads are imposed when cornering. It is the job of the suspension to counteract all these forces. And springs alone cannot do that.

THE FRONT WHEELS:

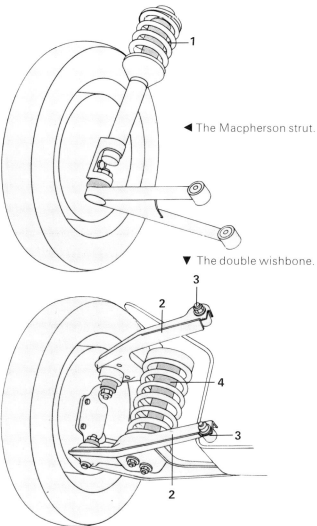

◀ The Macpherson strut.

▼ The double wishbone.

Macpherson strut

Like steering components, the suspension must be rigidly secure and free of wear to perform efficiently. On this system, first inspect the mountings on top of the inner wings under the bonnet for cracks and corrosion, for it is here that the forces are absorbed. Also examine the damper units inside the coil springs (1) for oil leaks (another damper check is to press down hard on each front wing: the car should only bounce up once before coming to rest). If all isn't well with any of these, seek garage advice.

Double wishbone

On this system, the coil spring and damper assembly is secured between two arms attached to the chassis. It is important to ensure that there is no movement in the bearings. A simple test is to lever between each wishbone (2) and its chassis mounting (3). If there is movement, suspect worn bushes, so have them looked at by an expert. Also examine the damper (4) for oil leaks. Do these same checks on single wishbone systems.

61

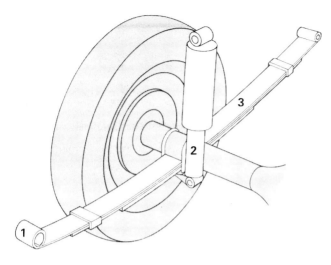

▲ The Hotchkiss drive comprises a rigid axle with leaf springs at each end. Wheel hub mountings, axle shafts and final drive are a single unit.

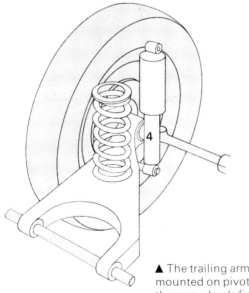

▲ The trailing arm design, mounted on pivots, holds the rear wheels firmly in situ, but allows them to move up and down.

THE REAR WHEELS:
Hotchkiss drive

In this system, semi-elliptic leaf springs are positioned at the extremities of the rear axle and, for shock absorption, the assembly is completed by telescopic dampers. Start your inspection by ensuring that all bolts securing the clamps around the spring leaves are tight. Next, move on to the rubber bump stops and straps, if fitted. If worn, damaged, oil fouled or perished, have them renewed. Now check for play in the rubber bushes at the point where the front end of the springs joins the chassis (1): lever between the spring and the bush, then between the spring and the shackle at the rear end chassis mounting point. In the event of up and down movement, seek garage advice. Also inspect the dampers (2) for leaks, and the spring leaves (3) for fractures.

Trailing arm design

There are several types of rear suspension. On this one arms, hinged at 90 degrees to the chassis, support each wheel. The dampers (4) should be checked (as above), and all parts examined for excessive wear and play, in which case seek garage advice.

The double wishbone is also used in some independent suspension systems. This differs from the frontal type in that its broad base is nearer the wheel. There is also a tie rod to cope with fore and aft loads.

Hydrogas suspension

Unlike conventional suspension systems which consist of springs and dampers, the hydrogas principle embodied in some models such as the one illustrated below comprises special cylinders filled with fluid and gas. Each roadwheel is linked to a cylinder by an arm, and the system is in two parts. A pipe links the front and rear cylinders on each side.

In this system, when the front wheel hits a bump, the arm moves a piston in the cylinder. This does two things: it compresses hydraulic fluid against a layer of gas which damps the shock, and forces the fluid through the pipeline to the rear cylinder which raises the car's back end. The same things happen in reverse when the rear wheel hits a bump. In this way, any fore-and-aft rocking motion is minimized, providing passengers with a more level ride.

Check the whole system occasionally for fluid loss, especially the cylinder displacer units and the pipeline joints. If there are any leaks, seek garage advice.

Citroën suspension

Certain Citroën cars have boasted hydro-pneumatic suspension for several years. When a wheel rises, this system too works on the principle of an arm activating a piston, which forces fluid in a spherical casing against a layer of gas, separated by a diaphragm. As the wheel falls, the reverse action takes place. Each wheel is connected to an individual sphere, which is fed by a fluid reservoir. There is also a load-levelling device operated by a slide valve.

▲ The main advantage of a linked system like the hydrogas suspension is that it significantly lessens any pitching tendency. The concept replaces both springs and dampers.

Servicing

A new concept in car maintenance, begun by BP Oil, means that owners no longer have to book their vehicles in for a complete garage service at the prescribed intervals. They can now do part of the work themselves and leave the difficult tasks to professional engineers. The following nine pages show the jobs that are within the capability of the average motorist.

Engine service

1. Check air cleaner element/replace.
2. Check fanbelt tension.
3. Check ignition system and timing.
4. Test/adjust/replace spark plugs and leads as required.
5. Check/adjust valve clearances.
6. Clean/test crankcase breather valve (if fitted).
7. Clean/replace engine breather filter (if fitted).
8. Check/renew servo filter element (if fitted).

Cooling/heating

9. Top-up radiator/system reservoir.
10. Check anti-freeze content.
11. Check systems for leaks.

Fuel system service

12. Check carburettor operation.
13. Check fuel pump filter and seal.
14. Check fuel injection system for: operation, timing, leaks.
15. Check visually fuel lines/unions for chafing/corrosion.
16. Check air/fuel ratio.
17. Check emission control (if fitted).

Brakes and clutch

18. Test brake and clutch operation — adjust as required.
19. Check for leaks and chafing all pipes/unions/hoses.
20. *Check brake pads/linings/drums, remove dust.
21. Check handbrake operation — adjust as required.
   *Mark hub/wheel positions for correct replacement and balance.

Lubrication

22. Change engine oil — apply oil grade sticker.
23. Renew oil filter.
24. Top-up gearbox/automatic transmission.
25. Top-up rear axle.
26. Top-up steering box/power steering/idler.
27. Lubricate steering rack and pinion.
28. Lubricate dynamo bearing.
29. Lubricate water pump.
30. Lubricate distributor mechanism.
31. Lubricate carburettor linkage and dashpot damper.
32. Lubricate all mechanical linkages/cables/pedal fulcrums.
33. Lubricate wheel bearings/hubs (see manufacturer's guide).
34. Lubricate all grease points.
35. Lubricate door, bonnet, boot hinges/fasteners.
36. Top up brakes and clutch reservoirs.

Body and underbody

37. Check for rust.
38. Check seat belts/anchorages/seat security.
39. Check/report condition of driving mirrors.
40. Check bonnet, body and door catches.
41. Check sun roof, clean drain channels.
42. Check exhaust system for leaks.
43. Check exhaust system anchorages.
44. Examine propeller shaft couplings/joints.
45. Examine springs and shock absorbers.
46. Check all retaining bolts for tightness.

Electrical equipment

47. Top-up battery/test/check cradle.
48. Clean and grease terminals.
49. Check lamps/flashers/horns for operation and alignment.
50. Check windscreen wiper operation and blades.
51. Check windscreen washers.
52. Check dynamo/alternator mountings.
53. Check starter motor operation.

Steering and wheels

54. Check wheel alignment.
55. Check wheel nuts for tightness.

56. Check all tyres for wear/ damage/specification.
57. Examine steering unit for leaks.
58. Examine ball joints, bushes and couplings.
59. Check front wheel bearings.
60. Check column retaining and clamp bolts.
61. Check air conditioning system (if fitted) for operation, leaks, damage and corrosion.

Items to leave to garage

Only 18 of the 61 schedules on the BP Oil service chart opposite are beyond the scope of the average motorist, and are therefore only listed and not explained in this book. However, do remember that we are concerned with checking and maintenance, and not adjustments, replacements and repairs which, because most are not within the capability of the majority of owners, should be dealt with by a garage.

The servicing items on the BP Oil list which should only be attended to by a trained mechanic are: Nos 3, 5, 6, 7, 8, 12, 13, 14, 16, 17, 18, 23, 33, 53, 54, 59, 60, 61.

Everything else on the schedule is within the scope of most owner-drivers and, if done at home, can represent a substantial financial saving.

Carburettor air cleaner

The commonest type(s) (shown in the next column) have one or two replaceable paper elements, depending on the number of carburettors. First remove the bolt or wing nut on top of the air cleaner body, detach the casing from the carburettor, then lift out the element. Lightly tap it to get out the dust and clean the container, the underside of the cover, and air intake. Refit the element, ensuring that the cleanest area faces the point

where the air enters. If, after tapping, the element is still clogged, replace it.

Some air cleaners have mesh filters bathed in oil. Remove the bolt or wingnut on top of the casing, detach the whole unit from the carburettor, then take out the element, which should be washed in petrol. Next, thoroughly clean the element bowl and refill with clean engine oil to the indicated level. Dry the element with a clean fluff-free cloth, and refit the assembly.

Some cars have cleaners which cannot be completely dissembled. These should be unclipped from the carburettor and held upside-down while petrol is poured into the air intake, swilled round and ejected.

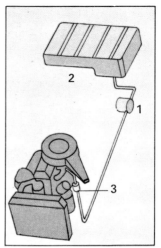

Fuel system

Occasionally check the petrol pump filter and seal, that is, if your car is fitted with a mechanical pump which you will find bolted to the side of the engine block. If, however, your vehicle has the kind of fuel system illustrated, in which an electric pump (1) draws petrol from the tank (2), the examination should be carried out by a garage. An in-line filter (3) can only be replaced by a new unit.

Only check mechanical pumps when the engine is cold. On types with a fuel line attached to the top cover, first disconnect the petrol pipe. Next, as with most types which do not have a fuel line attached to the top cover, undo the top nut or clip and take off the top. Remove the washer (replace if perished), then the filter gauze (wash this in petrol), and clean any particles from the filter housing.

Lubrication

A car is a machine, and like all things mechanical, its working parts need lubrication if they are to perform efficiently. Of course, the car is far more complex than other domestic machinery. Although manufacturers have devized methods to reduce the number of lubrication points, there are still some which need regular attention.

With the trend towards service-free components, car lubrication has become much less of a chore in recent years. Intervals between servicing have increased, too.

This has been the manufacturers' solution to encourage owners to maintain their cars. Unhappily, because there is no way fresh lubricant can be injected into many components the result is often a bill for a new part when something goes wrong.

But some systems, like those highlighted below, still require oil to be replenished (refer to your car handbook for the recommended service frequencies).

NB — On most modern cars, only checking the oil levels and topping up the gearbox and rear axle is necessary. If, however, an oil change has to be carried out, follow the procedures described in this section.

The engine

To drain and replace the engine oil, first switch on the engine for a few minutes then, after turning it off, remove the oil filler cap (1). Next, ascertain the sump capacity (it's in the handbook), and ensure that your collection container can cope. Now locate and remove the sump drain plug (2) with a spanner, screw-

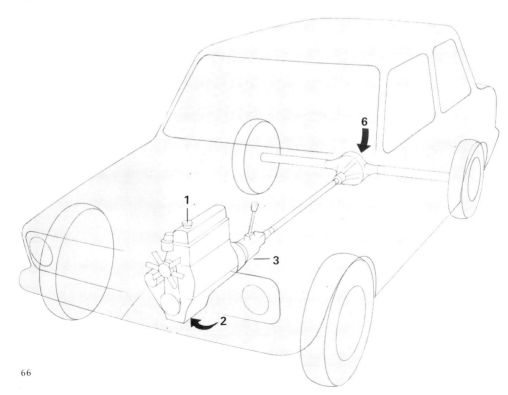

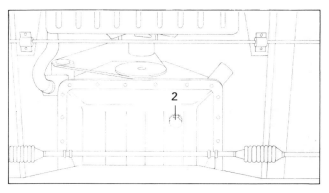

mended automatic transmission fluid and make sure that the funnel or container is scrupulously clean.

The rear axle

To drain the oil from the differential, first ensure that your collection container can take the amount which is given in the handbook. Then locate and remove the drain plug (4). After the old oil has been evacuated, replace the drain plug. Next locate and remove the filler plug (5) and, using the correct grade of oil, refill the differential with a plastic dispenser with a tube attached to it. Fill to the level of the filler hole (some differentials do not have drain plugs, but nonetheless require topping up). When topping up either type, be alert for a significant oil level drop, in which case suspect a damaged seal or gasket, and have the trouble rectified.

driver or special tool and drain the oil into the container (allow ten minutes). Replace the drain plug and, with a cloth, clean around the oil filler cap and, as below, pour in the correct grade and amount of oil (see handbook). Replace the filler cap. Turn on the engine and allow ten seconds for the oil warning light to go out or the pressure to register on the gauge. Should this not happen, switch off and have the trouble investigated.

(check the handbook for the amount), and preferably drain while the oil is warm. After draining, refit the drain plug, then clean the area around the filler plug (usually on the side of the gearbox). Remove this plug and replenish with the correct grade of fresh oil which will need to be dispensed with a plastic container with a tube at the top. Fill to the bottom of the filler hole. In between services, check the level occasionally, and top up if necessary. If there is serious loss, have it investigated.

On some cars, it is necessary to refill through the dipstick hole and, for this, you will need a funnel. If the aperture is hard to get at, use a plastic container with a tube at the top. Pour in sufficient oil to reach the high mark on the dipstick.

If your car has an automatic gearbox, follow the details in the handbook closely. Often, it has to be allowed to tick over for a time and then left standing for a while before a true reading can be obtained on the dipstick. When topping up, use only the recom-

The gearbox

Locate and remove the drain plug (3) (on the underside of the gearbox), first ensuring that your collection container has sufficient capacity

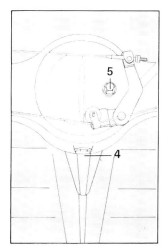

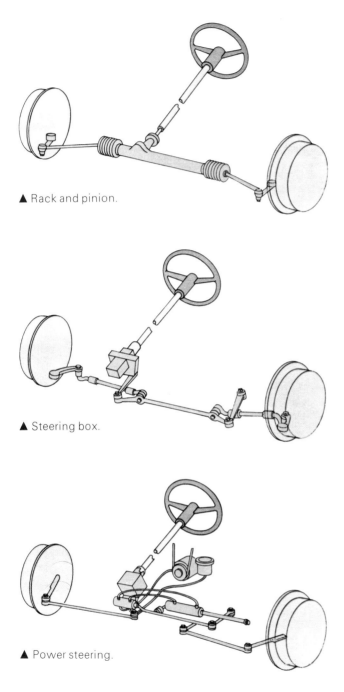

Lubricating rack and pinion steering

Refer to your car handbook to see if the assembly requires oil or grease, and carry out the manufacturer's instructions. In the event of a leak having been put right on an oil-filled type it must be re-filled. Loosen the clip on the gaiter at the driver's side, insert the spout of the oilcan into the opening and inject no more than 19 cl ($\frac{1}{3}$ pint) of the correct lubricant (see handbook).

▲ Rack and pinion.

Steering box

Refer to the handbook for the location of the steering box and the oil level plug, if fitted. Clean, then remove the plug and top up with the correct grade. If regular filling is required, seek garage advice. Also locate the idler on the opposite side, if fitted, and follow your handbook's instructions if it needs topping up with oil or grease. On oil types, check for leaks, which should be rectified by a garage.

▲ Steering box.

Power steering

Locate the power steering reservoir, and clean the area around the filler cap. Remove the cap and, if fitted, check the level on the dipstick, topping up if necessary. If there is no dipstick, top up to slightly above the filter pressure plate visible through the filler aperture. Check the level frequently: regular topping-up suggests a leak in the system which will require rapid professional attention.

▲ Power steering.

The dynamo

Some dynamos need occasional lubrication of the bearing, otherwise the bronze bush suffers premature wear and the generator becomes less efficient. Locate the relevant hole in the protruding end of the rear bush casing (see below), and inject three drops of light machine oil into it. N.B. — Over-lubrication can do irreparable harm.

Throttle linkage

Lubrication of the throttle linkage is a job that is all too easily forgotten. With a can of light machine oil, first lubricate the accelerator pedal shaft around the point where the pedal pivots. Next, on cable-operated mechanisms, thoroughly oil the cable leading from the pedal and, working the pedal by hand, make sure that the lubricant gets into the cable casing.

The dashpot damper

This is another neglected task. First clean the top of the carburettor suction chamber, unscrew the cap and take out the damper (1), see below. Refer to the car handbook for the recommended lubricant and fill to 7mm ($\frac{1}{4}$ in) below the top of the suction piston guide rod (2). Finally return the assembly and screw back the cap.

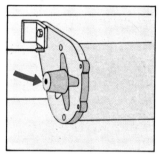

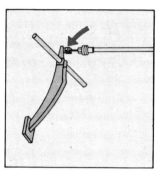

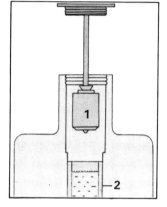

The water pump

Check the handbook to see if grease or oil should be used. If there is a nipple (as below), continue pumping until grease comes out of the side hole. Some systems have a blank plug which will have to be swapped for a nipple for the operation. If the lubrication point has a screw, remove it and inject a few drops of engine oil.

Then oil every pivot point on the cable and on the carburettor to which it is joined. Some cars are fitted with a pivot plate, one arm of which is connected by a cable to the pedal, and the other linked by a separate cable to the carburettor. This should be well lubricated.

Other jobs

Clutch linkage: as with the throttle linkage, lubricate the pedal shaft, cable and all pivot points.

Distributor lubrication: remove the top of the distributor and follow the car handbook's instructions.

Dynamo/alternator mountings: check the retaining bolts for tightness.

Anti-freeze: keep handy a correctly-balanced mixture for topping up.

Battery: occasionally clean and smear the terminals with petroleum jelly.

Jack: occasionally grease.

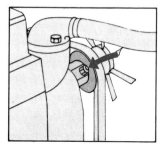

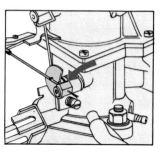

For your own good

Before tackling any dirty job on the car, even if only changing a wheel, apply barrier cream liberally to the hands and forearms, especially knuckles and nails. This will make the job of cleaning off oil and grime very much easier later.

If working under the car, also rub barrier cream on your face, ears and exposed parts of the neck. For good measure, wear something on your head and, to avoid getting oil and dust in your eyes, put on a pair of goggles.

When you have finished, remove the dirt with a proprietary petroleum jelly

▼ Greasing the front suspension.

cleaner and rinse off with water. Stubborn grime, particularly in fingernails, should be treated with a nailbrush soaked in paraffin.

Greasing has already been referred to (on pages 68-69) and the next section looks into this aspect of servicing in more detail. The first thing to check is whether you have the right grease gun for the nipples on your car. If not, you may have to buy an adaptor, so check this detail with a dealer specializing in your make and model before you set to work. Check the handbook for the grease you should use.

When you open a tin of grease, you will usually find a plate inside with a centre hole. Load the grease gun or cartridge by placing the

open end over this hole and pressing down.

Draining oil

No matter how careful you are with oil, spillage can occur, especially when draining. To prevent unsightly stains on the concrete floor of your garage or driveway, cover the affected areas immediately with sawdust or sand. Allow to soak before tidying up, then wash the floor. If stains persist, treat with a proprietary concrete cleaner.

Finally to the question of oil disposal. Don't threaten the environment by pouring it into a hole in the garden, and remember it's illegal to dump it down a drain. Take it to a garage, or seek advice from your local council.

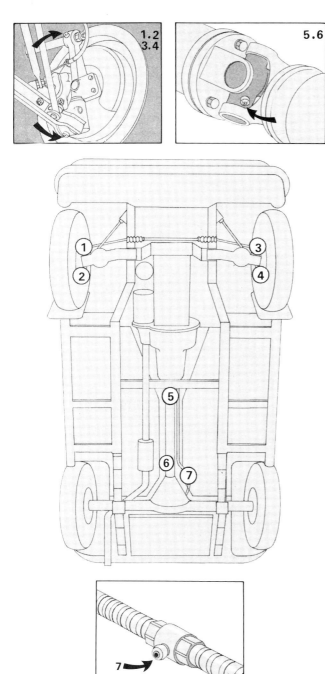

Greasing

On some cars there are still moving parts which need to be replenished with fresh grease (check with your car handbook for the points that require attention, and the type of grease recommended for each job).

Before pumping in the grease, clean the nipple with a cloth, then press the end of the grease gun on to it. Ensure positive contact and apply the number of strokes recommended for each item in the handbook.

If the grease splays out of the end of the gun and is obviously not going in, suspect a blockage. Unscrew the nipple, attach the gun to it and try and pump out the obstruction (on nipples without a valve, clear the blockage with a piece of stout wire). If this doesn't work, replace it with a new one of the same type.

The diagram illustrates the commonest grease points (1, 2, 3, 4). Rack and pinion steering: first tackle the nipple at the ball joint on the steering track rod end and attach the gun. Then locate the nipple on the lower swivel joint on the front stub axle.

On steering box and idler systems, locate the nipples on the ball joints, if fitted.

On universal joints (5 and 6), keep pumping until grease exudes from the joints. Also check for grease points on the handbrake cable system (7 is a popular location).

Body points

Few owners appreciate that bodywork parts need to be lubricated, too, that is, until something like a door lock seizes and they cannot get out of the car.

So start with the doors, first attending to the striker plates (1) on the centre pillars and rear door frames. If made of metal, apply a few drops of light machine oil; for nylon fittings, use a lubricant specially made for the job.

Also lubricate the exposed parts of the door locks (2) and check whether there is a small aperture around the mechanism. If so, squirt in a few drops of light machine oil.

In addition, lightly lubricate the door hinge pivots. But remember to remove surplus oil from all these mechanisms, otherwise you could face a dry cleaning bill!

The locks and hinges on the boot (3) and bonnet require occasional attention as well: again, using light machine oil, place a few drops on them and on the bonnet striker plate and pin (4).

For lubrication of sunshine roofs and rear luggage doors of hatchback and estate models, refer to the car handbook

Emergency repairs

Breakdowns are inconvenient at the best of times. Although lack of servicing is the most common reason for failures on the road, even the best-maintained car can suffer unexpected trouble. Breaking down can be expensive, too, if you have to call out a garage. Yet many of the things that garages are called out to deal with are of a comparatively minor nature which, for the want of the right spare part, tool or knowhow, the owner could fix himself in no time at all.'

Changing a wheel

It's incredible but true that even dealing with a puncture is beyond many drivers. Equally remarkable are the reasons: unserviceable spare tyres, for instance, insufficient tools, and perhaps the most common trouble of all: stubborn wheelnuts. So be prepared: make sure that the spare is alright, the jack works, that you have a wheelbrace and that all wheel studs are smeared with graphite grease so the nuts come off easier. Three last tips: loosen the wheelnuts before jacking, always jack on firm level ground, and if you find the spare wheel too heavy don't lift it out of the boot. Stand it on end and roll it like a hoop up to the boot rim, then lift it down.

Damp start

Rain, dew and condensation can play havoc with the ignition system, to the extent that the engine will simply refuse to start. Once again the motto is: be prepared. Have ready to hand a proprietary aerosol of water repellant specially made to keep moisture out of the system. As prevention is

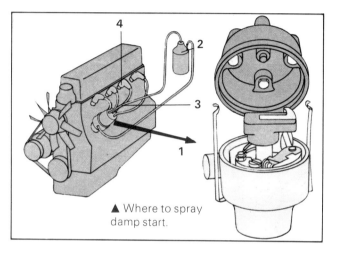

▲ Where to spray damp start.

always better than cure, listen to the weather forecast and lightly spray the distributor (1), coil (2), high tension leads (3) and sparking plugs (4) the night before (ready for the morning) or early in the evening (if you are returning home late).

Broken fanbelt

The first signs are the ignition warning light coming on while the car is in motion and a sudden rise of the temperature gauge. The easiest way to deal with the problem is to carry a temporary fanbelt which simply

slips over the pulleys. But remember: it is only a temporary 'get-you-home' remedy. Have a proper replacement fitted as soon as possible.

Flat battery

One sign of imminent battery failure is a sluggish starter motor. And if one day there is not enough charge left in it to turn the engine, you have no real problem, providing you have bought and have handy a set of jump leads. Simply ask another motorist for assistance and, with the red (+) cable clips, bridge the positive terminals of his battery and yours. The black (—) cable connects the negative terminals. But ensure that you fix the ends to the right terminals, otherwise you could do a lot of damage. Finally, get your helper to rev his engine while you operate the starter on your car.

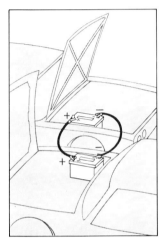

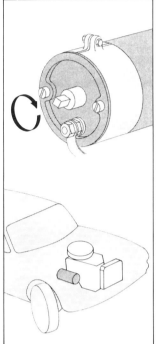

Jammed starter motor

If, when you switch on the engine, you hear a loud click and nothing else happens, suspect a jammed starter motor. Switch on your headlamps, operate the starter again and, if the lights go very dim, the trouble is almost certainly confirmed. First locate the starter motor, then find the squared end (see illustration). If hidden by a dust cover, remove this with the aid of a screwdriver. The starter motor can usually be freed by fitting a spanner over the squared end and turning clockwise. If the starter is faulty, con-

sider a push start (providing you haven't got automatic transmission, in which case seek garage advice). Sit behind the wheel and get two helpers to push the car. Switch on the ignition, select second gear, and keep the clutch pedal depressed. When a reasonable speed is reached, let out the clutch. If this doesn't do the trick, repeat until it does.

Boiling radiator

The first sign that all is not well is the needle of the temperature gauge climbing rapidly or the temperature warning light coming on. Finally, you will see steam coming from the front end.

As there are several possible causes, the immediate priority is to locate the source of the trouble.

Before stopping and switching off, check that the ignition warning light isn't on (if it is, suspect a broken or slipping fanbelt, in which case adjust or replace). Otherwise raise the bonnet then leave things for about 20 minutes.

Cover the radiator cap with a cloth and, keeping at arm's length, ease off the cap a half-turn at a time to avoid scalding. Check whether there is water in the tank. If not, inspect the system for leaks: check hoses for damage and tightness of the clips; look for radiator damage and test the security of the system's drain plugs (refer to the handbook). After remedying (unless the radiator is damaged, in which case you will require garage assistance), wait for the engine to cool right down before replenishing the system with water. Switch on the engine for a few minutes and watch the radiator tank level. If it remains topped up, replace the pressure cap and proceed on your way.

If you have a sealed cooling system, undo the plug at the top of the radiator when cool, and trickle in the water very slowly. When filled, replace the plug and switch on the engine for five minutes. Allow it to cool, then fill the expansion chamber to the recommended level. Run the engine for another five minutes and top up the expansion chamber as necessary. Repeat three or four times.

If the problem is a partially-frozen hose, you should be able to feel the ice by pinching the hose. Leave until it has thawed. If completely frozen, attempt to take off the hose. If this is impossible, consider cutting the hose with a hacksaw; the release of pressure could save the engine from damage.

Expect to be at the roadside for quite a while. Overheating is serious because it can badly harm the engine. Once again, the need to carry a full set of spare hoses, tools, a temporary or proper fanbelt, and a water container cannot be emphasized enough.

Towing

If repair is impossible, find a motorist willing to give you a tow to a garage. Considering the cost of a garage tow, the wisdom of carrying a tow rope is obvious.

Attach both ends to solid structural parts such as suspension mountings (see illustration below left), ensuring that the rope does not chafe bodywork or roadwheels. Towing and being towed isn't easy. The tower must change gear smoothly, use his brakes gently, and resort to hand signals in good time for the benefit of the driver being towed. Go slowly and keep the rope taut. N.B. If your car has servo-assisted brakes, you will need to press the pedal more firmly (assuming the engine isn't running). For towing of automatic transmission models, refer to your handbook.

Shattered windscreen

If you lose forward vision, firmly punch a hole through the windscreen, keeping your wrist and forearm straight. The brisker the blow, the less risk of cutting yourself. Pull off the road and remove the rest of the glass, protecting the bonnet with a blanket or something similar. Wrap the glass in the blanket and take it home with you for disposal. The precaution of having taken the trouble of buying and carrying an emergency windscreen (bottom) will be all too clear if it's cold, snowing or raining.

▼ Common towing points (1 the towed vehicle; 2 the towing vehicle.)

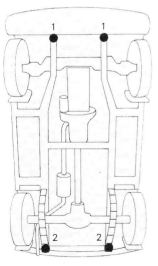

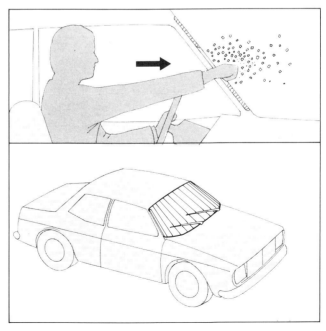

Economical driving

So far, we have concentrated our cost-cutting activities on the issues of frequent checks, regular maintenance and having everything to hand when you need it. There is another vital ingredient for economical car ownership: you. Or, more precisely, the way you drive. It's a fact that you can make your petrol go further with careful handling. But be warned, it won't be easy. Old habits can be hard to break but, if you can do it, it's worth it, especially when you tot up your savings over a year. There's another potential spin-off, too. You will almost certainly reduce the odds of being involved in an accident. And that, apart from your continued well-being, means more cash saved.

If you are not yet convinced that driving fast means significantly higher petrol consumption, consider the results of one eyebrow-raising experiment that took place just a few years ago.

Two family saloons set off together on the 900-mile journey from Hamburg to the Italian Adriatic resort of Rimini. The driver of Car A was briefed to motor as fast as he could. The man behind the wheel of Car B, on the other hand, was told to observe all speed restrictions to the letter and generally take things easy.

Remarkably, Car A arrived at the holiday town only half-an-hour ahead of its rival. And used nine gallons more petrol. As it turned out, that wasn't the only benefit the occupants of Car B enjoyed. Unlike the others, they stopped for refreshments on the way and were able to sit back and admire the scenery whereas the unfortunate driver of Car A took two days of his vacation to wind down.

When the road record of Car A is analyzed, the one thing that stands out is its speed performance which was extremely erratic. All the impetus it burned petrol to achieve was lost in hasty braking and tyre-squeal cornering. In fact, it braked sharply 682 times more than the other vehicle, made five emergency stops, and had to pause for ten minutes at one point through overheating.

Other trials have also shown just how much fuel consumption is affected by speed. The diagram opposite tells the story, illustrating in full measure the distance obtained at constant miles-per-hour on a gallon of fuel. An extension to this particular experiment, aimed at finding out how different driving techniques have a marked bearing on consumption, demonstrated that a gallon took the vehicle 20 miles when driven hard. Normal motoring achieved 26.5 miles, whereas very quiet driving yielded 32.7 miles.

It is sudden bursts of acceleration that really hit the pocket. A vehicle capable of attaining 37mpg at 30mph will barely take you nine miles if accelerated flat out from stop and maintained at top speed thereafter. Indeed, it has been calculated that you need as much fuel in the first 20 yards from standstill as you use to take you half a mile at 30mph.

Gently done

The key, then, to safe, econominical driving is smoothness. Nothing should be done in a hurry. Sudden changes of speed or direction can increase the strain on steering and transmission by up to 40 per cent. Fierce acceleration and racing up through the gears can only hasten the wearing-out process of the car and fray the nerves of its driver and passengers.

As the Hamburg-Rimini run clearly shows, harsh braking, invariably caused by excessive speed, is something else to be avoided. In

▼ Just how much speed affects consumption is shown by the performance of a 2 litre car at various speeds on one gallon of petrol.

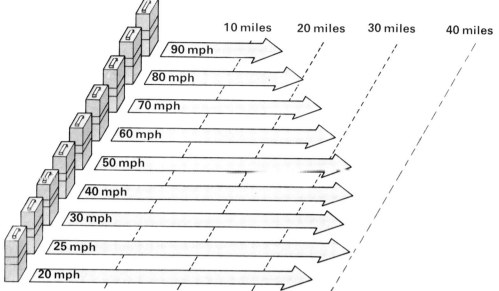

10 miles 20 miles 30 miles 40 miles

90 mph
80 mph
70 mph
60 mph
50 mph
40 mph
30 mph
25 mph
20 mph

addition to wasting the petrol you have used to reach that excessive speed, it increases brake and tyre wear.

Instead, consciously adjust your speed to the conditions with as little pressure on the throttle pedal as possible. If you react in good time to situations, you will hardly ever have to use the brake pedal, but simply take your foot off the accelerator.

Some further tips

How you corner is important too, if you really mean to cut your petrol and tyre replacement bills. On the approach, providing you have judged correctly, there should be no need to adjust speed by braking through the gears. Decelerate long before you reach the bend or

junction and bring down your speed with gentle applications of the brake pedal.

The art of gear changing, a real money-saver if carried out expertly, is a skill few drivers have, but it can be achieved if you work at it hard enough. Change gear only when the speed you have attained in a lower gear can be maintained without increased throttle in the next gear up. When changing down, avoid a loud, racing surge in engine speed.

When changing up, aim to get into top gear as soon as possible without labouring the engine.

Even before setting off on a journey, there is much you can do to prevent wear and the squandering of fuel. Avoid, for example, repeat-

edly using the starter in short bursts, as this habit can cause damage to the flywheel. If your model has a manual choke, return it progressively as the engine warms up. Excessive choke spells an over-rich mixture, which means wasted petrol. It can also lead to premature wear of the piston rings and cylinder bores.

Never rev the engine as soon as it starts; the oil hasn't had time to circulate properly, and this practice could put undue strain on a vital bearing through lack of lubrication.

Get in the habit, too, of moving off as soon as you start the engine. The engine will reach its efficient working temperature much more quickly when on the move.

Motoring howlers

Some of the strangest advice about driving and the way to treat the car is handed down from generation to generation. And most of it, far from being beneficial, couldn't be more wrong and, in some cases, downright harmful. Like: when a fuse goes and you haven't a spare, or your replacement fuses blow too, substitute a piece of aluminium foil. Just you try it and you could end up on fire. Here are some other gems of useless information that are commonly bandied about.

Blip and stop

Blipping the throttle pedal before turning off the engine is a practice not generally passed on by word of mouth, but by example. How many times have you travelled in someone else's car and, at the end of the run, the driver has done precisely this? Well, don't fall into the trap of copying him. Unvaporized petrol gets into the cylinders, washing the protective oil film from the bores. The same thing can happen if the throttle pedal is used when starting a warm engine. Such habits cause the pistons to run in dry bores, and this leads to premature piston ring and cylinder bore wear.

Choke and strangle

Pulling out the choke while driving along, some motorists are convinced, will make the car go faster. In fact, it will only accelerate engine wear. Exactly the same hap-

pens when the accelerator pedal is blipped before switching off the engine. It causes neat petrol to remove lubricant from the cylinder bores. And having pistons travelling in dry bores doesn't do the engine any good at all. The result, once again, is piston ring and cylinder bore wear. This is an expensive repair, so why do your utmost to encourage the damage? Leave the choke where it is. It's there for one purpose only: to help you to start the engine when it's cold.

How to remove your gearbox

'The best way to push or bump start a car is in reverse gear.' Whoever dreamed up this advice was himself guilty of getting his facts back-to-front. He obviously worked out that, as reverse is the lowest gear on a car, a successful push start could be achieved at a much lower speed. In fact, second gear is best. Reverse gears, or even first on some cars, have such low ratios that damage can be caused to the gears or drive shafts.

Supercar

'Filling up with a higher octane petrol than the grade

recommended by the manufacturer will not only make the car go faster, but give you better fuel consumption.' This, too, is a popular misconception. All you will end up doing is paying more than you need for petrol. A car's power output is not restricted to the volatility of the fuel alone, but also to the amount of air that can be compressed and heated.

Good braking

'A sign of good brakes is that all four wheels lock on directly the pedal is applied'. However logical the notion might seem on paper, just

try it in practice, especially in the wet! Another danger is that the brakes may be more efficient on one side than the other, which could cause the car to veer viciously with disastrous results even in the dry. The problem is confined to vehicles with drum brakes all round. And over-adjustment can cause prematurely worn linings and brake fade.

Rust improver

'If you haven't a garage, your car will last longer if you cover it with a tarpaulin.' Oh yes? Make a regular habit of this and you will end up damaging the paintwork by grinding in minute grit particles every time you put the tarpaulin on or take it off. And if the material is not ventilated, condensa-

tion inside and hot sun outside positively invites rust.

Tightening your belt

'The tighter you adjust the fanbelt, the better the performance you will get from the dynamo or alternator, and water pump.' Overtightening can cause pre-

mature failure of the belt and bearings. Leave 20mm ($\frac{3}{4}$in.) play in the longest run of the belt between pulleys on a

dynamo system, and very slight slack on an alternator system.

Radiator omelet?

'A radiator leak? No trouble. Shove a tinful of mustard down the filler hole. Or dried soup, oatmeal or raw eggs!' Maybe in the old days the remedy worked, the idea being that the substance would solidify at the leak and effect a seal. The snag is that today's coolant systems are pressurized and the seal simply won't hold.

Breakdown chart

1. Starter will not turn engine and the headlamps go dim

There are three possible problems: a jammed starter motor, loose or corroded battery terminals, or a flat battery. Finding out which of these is the cause is a matter of trial and error. If the starter motor has stuck, you will almost certainly hear a loud click each time you turn the key in the ignition lock. Refer to page 74 for the remedy, and if this doesn't do the trick go on to the battery, take off the terminals and clean these and the battery posts with fine emery cloth. Then refit tightly. Also clean the connection of the braided strap with the car body. If the starter motor still doesn't turn, then resort to jump leads (see page 74). And if that doesn't succeed, you will need garage assistance.

2. Starter will not turn engine and the headlamps stay bright

Before calling for professional assistance, ensure that the gear is in neutral, switch on the ignition and try activating the solenoid under the bonnet (refer to your car handbook for its location). Some have a manual button, so press it and see. Don't touch the solenoid, however, if it's fixed to the starter motor.

3. Engine turns but will not start

The first priority is to determine whether current is reaching the sparking plugs. So remove all the plugs, then reconnect the lead to one of them, and place it against bare metal. Now, switch on the ignition and, manually turning the top fanbelt pulley, turn the engine at least one revolution. If no spark is produced by the plug, suspect a damp ignition system (see page 73 for the remedy) or look for loose or disconnected leads.

If there is a good spark, make sure that you have petrol. If so, check that the ventilation hole in the fuel filler cap isn't obstructed. Next ensure that the engine is not suffering from excess fuel: operate the starter with the accelerator fully depressed. If this doesn't work, remove the sparking plugs, dry and replace. A clogged petrol filter is another possible cause (see page 65).

4. Brakes pull to one side

The most evident reason is a soft tyre on one side, so check the pressures and change the wheel if necessary. This trouble is also symptomatic of worn or contaminated brake linings, but examining and maybe replacing these at the roadside is scarcely practical.

5. Loss of braking after a long descent

This indicates brake fade caused by overheating of the system, so allow to cool. Two other causes could be worn linings or that the brake fluid needs changing: if so, seek garage advice without delay. It is frights like this that emphasize the importance of checking the brakes and following the manufacturer's recommendations on replacing the hydraulic fluid. Most drivers never give a second thought to the fluid, but it is vital that they do. For the system absorbs water and, if this is allowed to build up, vapour lock can occur and prevent the brakes from working.

6. Grinding noise from the wheels

This is probably due to one of two things — binding brakes or dry wheel bearings. It is possible to adjust the brakes yourself on some cars (refer to the car handbook) but it can be a fiddly task and may be best left to a garage. Lubrication of the wheel bearings, especially after being allowed to run dry, is definitely a job for the professional, for the bearings will probably have to be dismantled.

7. Oil warning light stays on when engine is running

This indicates very low oil pressure, and you should stop the car at once. The first thing to do is to check the engine oil level on the dipstick, but ensure that the car is on level ground and wait a few minutes to allow the oil to drain into the sump. Don't proceed on your way until the cause has been put right and the oil topped up.

8. Oil light flashes when cornering

This is a sure sign that the engine oil level is low. Check the level on the dipstick and top up as necessary.

9. Ignition warning light stays on above idling speed

Suspect a slipping or broken fanbelt, or trouble in the area of the generator — for it means that the battery isn't charging. Inspect the fanbelt first and, if still present, check for tightness. On a dynamo system, there should be about 20mm ($\frac{3}{4}$ in) play on the longest length of belt between two of the pulleys. On an alternator system, the slack on the longest run between pulleys should be slight. Readjust or replace as necessary. If the problem appears to be in the dynamo itself or the alternator, seek garage advice.

10. Temperature gauge climbs then drops to cold

This is indicative of loss of coolant, overheating . . . or both. Pull off the road as soon as possible, otherwise serious engine damage could result. Switch off the engine and raise the bonnet. For safety, allow 20 minutes to cool then, holding a cloth at arm's length, undo the radiator pressure cap half a turn at a time. Now refer to page 74.

Don't be misled by the temperature gauge needle going to cold. Once coolant has been lost, there is nothing to conduct heat to the sensor.

11. Burning smells

If you miss the initial rise of temperature on the gauge (see section 10), the next warning is a hot smell as paint and oil become heated. But the trouble could be wires shorting out, too, in which case disconnect the battery without delay and get garage assistance. Oil or rag on the exhaust could be another reason.

12. Petrol smells

The main thing you need to be wary of is, of course, a leak which will need to be located immediately and rectified. Another cause could be the carburettor flooding which, if it persists without due cause, is a job for a specialist.

13. Fast clicking sound from an electric fuel pump

The commonest reason is that the car has been standing in hot weather and the petrol up to the carburettor has evaporated. But it could also be caused by a shortage of fuel in the tank. Or an air lock between the tank and the pump, the remedy for which is to tighten the petrol pipe joints.

14. Steering vibration

If you have recently taken off a wheel, this could be the cause — if you didn't mark a hole and its corresponding wheelstud to ensure that the wheel went on exactly the same way as it came off, it could be out of balance. Another cause could be that a balancing weight has dropped off — either way, the car will have to go to a garage to have the wheels balanced. Also check that the wheelnuts are tight.

15. Engine speed increases when climbing hills at a steady rate

This is almost certainly clutch slip. On some cars, a garage adjustment will do the trick. But more often than not it means a new friction disc, or that oil has seeped on to the linings — either way it's a job for a specialist.

How to diagnose

If the brakes start to judder, suspect distorted drums or discs, the wrong or worn linings, or even dust. A brake overhaul at the earliest opportunity is the only answer.

Brake squeal? Again, the wrong or worn linings, or dust are the probable causes. Check and clean.

A bubbling sound after the engine has been switched off almost certainly means overheating. Once the cooling system has cooled down, check it.

Perhaps there's a screeching noise from the front of the engine. The likeliest sources are a slipping fanbelt, a frozen water pump, or a dry bearing in the generator or water pump. The respective remedies are: rectify fanbelt tension or replace, allow the water pump to thaw out and, referring to the car handbook, lubricate the two bearings sparingly.

If your car clanks when taking up the load, the possible reasons are a worn universal joint on the propshaft, a worn, or leaking loose rear axle, or insufficient oil in the gearbox. A worn universal joint is a garage job, but you can check the gearbox and axle oil levels yourself. However, if topping up and tightening the drain plugs doesn't do the trick, be prepared to have the trouble sorted out by an expert.

Another sound to give you that sinking feeling is a grinding noise when the clutch is depressed. The cause is probably a worn clutch release bearing or spigot bush. Either way it will mean a clutch overhaul at a garage.

A whirring noise that stops when the clutch is depressed is, thankfully, not so drastic. The chances are that the source is the constant mesh gears in the gearbox - as long as the oil level is all right, there isn't usually anything to worry about.

But a heavy knock under acceleration can be very bad news. This almost certainly means a worn big end bearing, and an expensive repair to pay for.

A heavy rumbling when the engine is under load is symptomatic of worn main bearings and, again, is one of the most unwelcome eventualities. For, once more, the usual remedy is a reconditioned engine.

Buying a car

It's a small detail, but one that many forget when setting out to buy a new or secondhand car. The result, when you drive the vehicle into your garage for the first time and discover to your horror that you can't open a door to get out, can be splendid entertainment for the neighbours. But needless distress and embarrassment to yourself. So remember to measure the dimensions of the garage first.

The next step is to decide to what use the car is going to be put. A snazzy sports car can be the envy of the street, but just try getting a couple of children, a pram and the shopping in it as well as you and your partner. So take everything into consideration, and be practical.

And being practical also means deciding what you can afford. A common pitfall is to forget all about the overheads – putting the car on the road (tax, insurance etc.), the running costs, and the one thing most fail to include in the reckoning: keeping some cash by to afford the inevitable replacements (tyres, battery etc) and repair bills. So don't spend the whole of the budget on the vehicle's asking price.

Tread warily, too, if you take out hire purchase: ensure that you can keep up the repayments otherwise, like dozens of others every week of the year, you'll suddenly find your car reclaimed and sold off by the finance company.

Without doubt, the cheapest method of buying a car is with ready cash. Any means of extended payment means additional costs – especially with the high rates of interest these days.

Of the avenues open to you for credit, probably the best is a loan arrangement from an insurance company – providing that you already have an endowment policy.

Otherwise, you might consider borrowing from a financial company – particularly if you belong to the AA or RAC. Both organizations offer preferential interest arrangements to members.

Choosing your car

If your annual mileage is likely to be high, a new car is the best solution, for faults will probably occur in the warranty period which means not all of the cost to put them right will come out of your pocket. And as the most expensive single everyday item will almost certainly be petrol, it will pay you to forsake the extra comforts of a big car and think of a smaller model that will give you a lot more miles per gallon.

If on the other hand, you expect your yearly mileage to be on the low side, a secondhand vehicle is probably the best decision. But regardless of its price, think seriously of having it checked by a qualified engineer, preferably from the Automobile Association or the Royal Automobile Club. The comparatively small fee involved could save you a lot of money later on.

Don't just follow the trend of buying foreign for the sake of it without careful consideration. Products from overseas have as many shortcomings as those made in Britain, and often in the same areas. But it is a curious fact of life that customers expect more of a home-produced model than one made elsewhere. Another thing to bear in mind is the shortage of some foreign parts. They invariably cost more, too.

If you do elect to buy a new car, and you intend to keep it for a long while, think seriously of having the vehicle rust-proofed by a firm that specializes in such treatments. And have it done right away.

If you buy secondhand, go to a reputable dealer. Buying from a private seller or at a car auction might, on paper, seem a cheaper exercise. But your chances of buying a load of trouble are much increased. What is more, these sources don't offer a guarantee. A reputable dealer, on the other hand, has his reputation to protect, and if he is a main dealer for one of the big manufacturers, there is a good chance that the used models on the forecourt have been checked in the workshops. Two other advantages of going to a reputable dealer are that you stand a chance of having bits and pieces you may not be satisfied with replaced for nominal or no cost (as long as you bring them to his attention before purchase), and obtaining a good trade-in deal on the car you are running at the moment.

New or secondhand, look carefully before you spend your money.

Useful addresses:

Motor Agents Association,
201 Great Portland Street,
London W1N 6AB.
Society of Motor Manufacturers and Traders,
Forbes House,
Halkin Street,
London SW1X 7DS.
Scottish Motor Trade Association,
3 Palmerston Place,
Edinburgh EH12 5AQ.

Getting on the road

Having bought your car, the first step is to make sure that you are legally entitled to take it out on to the road. To do so, you must have a valid driving licence, a current and valid road excise fund licence, displayed in the lower nearside corner of the windscreen, and registration document bearing the correct details of the car (both are obtainable from the Vehicle Licensing Centre, Swansea), the correct registration plates (if the car is brand-new), a current MOT test certificate (if the vehicle is more than three years old) and a certificate of insurance.

There's not a great deal that you can do about the other requirements to economize, but by shopping around for insurance you can save yourself a lot of money.

Another basic essential, if you have purchased a new car, is to go over it with a fine toothcomb when taking delivery. Don't take it for granted that it will be perfect just because it has come straight out of the showroom.

Be especially alert to paint damage. Remember: the quicker you bring blemishes to a dealer's attention, the easier it will be to have them put right.

Insurance

First, however, a word on the types of insurance available. The most basic is called Road Traffic Act insurance which merely covers your legal liability for the death or injury of any person caused by the car. However, this kind of policy is so fundamental that all other liability – repairing any damage you may cause – comes out of your pocket.

Although premiums are higher, third-party policies afford much more protection: in addition to the cover provided by the basic Road Traffic Act insurance, they include pay-out arrangements in respect of other people's property, and extensions are available to cover your own vehicle for fire and theft.

Third-party, though, does not reimburse you for any damage your own car may sustain in a collision. For that, you will need to take out a comprehensive policy. And because the benefits are greater, the premiums are obviously more expensive.

The 'extras' include the payment of a lump sum if the policyholder or spouse is killed or injured in any car, and compensation for any personal possessions stolen from the insured vehicle.

Shopping around not only saves you money: different companies offer different protection. So it's worth studying as many brochures as possible to see what you get for your money and to compare notes before committing yourself.

As a guide, among the sort of things you should be looking for are: high compensation for the loss of limbs and eyes; cover for other members of the family; good medical expenses; compensation for loss of or damage to accessories and possessions; an arrangement whereby a stolen car under a year old is replaced with a new vehicle, and free car hire is available while your car is being repaired; a clause which means you don't have to pay towing and redelivery charges if your car has to be taken away for accident repairs; and windscreen breakage cover, for which there is no loss of no-claim discount.

No-claim discount arrangements need careful scrutiny. Look not only for good terms, but also for insurances under which the maximum discount is protected even in the event of claims within a certain period.

Don't forget the other discounts, either. Undertakings like voluntary damage excess, and restricting the driving of the car to yourself and one other person can reduce the cost of the premium. Even the nature of your occupation can reduce the premium.

But whatever you do, make sure you fill in the proposal form 100 per cent accurately. If you don't, the company can use this as grounds to reject a claim. Be especially careful when answering questions about other drivers you wish to be covered to drive your car. Make a point of questioning them on their past driving record. If they have had a conviction, or have been involved in an accident, then notify the insurer. Also inform the company straightaway if any circumstances, described in the original proposal, change for some reason.

So don't sit back and wait for the insurers to send you the next renewal form before telling them about that speeding fine and licence endorsement, or whatever. It could mean the difference between having a claim met and having it turned down.

And, take note, some companies reserve the right of withholding a pay-out if your car hasn't been maintained properly.

Driving courses

Perhaps you haven't learned to drive yet. Or someone in the family is just coming up to the age when they will be able to take lessons. The big question is: who should provide the tuition?

The first thought that crosses many people's minds is to get a friend or relative to teach them – a notion that becomes increasingly attractive when the going hourly rate charged by driving schools is considered.

The trouble is that most drivers, since passing their tests, have developed bad habits which are all too easily passed on.

By all means, use friends and relatives to obtain valuable practice, but not instruction. That comes from only one source: a qualified driving instructor.

Choosing a good one, however, is something else. Personal recommendations are best – from friends or acquaintances who have recently cast aside their L-plates. Failing that, contact an official of your local area driving instructors' association (the public library should be able to give you details), or your regional road safety office.

Once you have met the instructor of your choice, don't be afraid to ask him or her for proof of their qualifications. Professional tutors have to be officially approved by the Department of Transport by law,

and should carry a certificate to this effect. This is an important precaution, because a number of so-called driving instructors are operating illegally.

Also, if you have the option, limit your practice to one type of car – preferably the same type used by the driving school. Driving widely-differing models at the start can hinder your learning.

Another word of warning: just because you pass your test doesn't mean you're a driver. It merely indicates that you have grasped the basic essentials. If you really mean to become a driver, read the rest of this page and the next.

There are two organizations that run advanced driving tests: the Institute of Advanced Motorists and the League of Safe Drivers. One very good reason to pass their theory and practical exams is that successful candidates can obtain insurance discounts.

And if you look hard enough, you can try your hand at skid control. There aren't many public skidpans and skid circuits around but, if you can get along to one, it is money well spent.

Skidding

Two seconds elapse before the average motorist takes evasive action in a skid situation – and, by then, it's too late. In that time, at just 45mph, a driver will have travelled across six lanes of motorway and halfway back again.

But three hours of tuition and practice, and a refresher course once a year, will teach you to respond instinctively and correctly in the split second a skid begins.

The courses also get you braking and steering properly. And they improve your driving to the extent that you probably won't even get into a skid in the

first place.

The fact that, each year in Britain, skidding alone accounts for 70,000 casualties tends to demonstrate many drivers still have an awful lot to learn.

And with an increasing number of moped and motor-cycle riders taking to the roads without tuition, it is perhaps timely, in the light of the alarming number of accidents involving two-wheelers, to direct their attention to the fact that courses do exist. Many boroughs run RAC/ACU training schemes, so get in touch with your local road safety office.

Skid pans

The following skidpans are open to the public by appointment:

Crystal Palace Driver Education Centre, London SE19 (01-659 1727).

Kensington Road, Ealing, London W5 (01-845 4460).

Brands Hatch Motor Racing Circuit, Fawkham, Kent (01-352 1014).

Miller's Driving Centre, Goodwood Circuit, Chichester, Sussex (Chichester 84715).

Tempsford Airfield near Sandy, Beds. (clubs and groups only: Bedford 6322).

Thruxton Driver Education Centre, near Andover, Hants. (01-659 1727).

Jim Russell Skid Control School, Snetterton Circuit, Norfolk (Quidenham 451).

Tamworth School of Motoring, Staffs. (Tamworth 62669).

For details of advanced driving tests, contact:

The Institute of Advanced Motorists, Empire House, Chiswick High Road, London W4.

The League of Safe Drivers, 17 Holmwood Gardens, London N3 3NS.

Other courses

With the increasing popularity of evening classes for adults, it's perhaps scarcely surprising that car maintenance and repair courses are proliferating. In these days of high labour rates, do-it-yourself vehicle mechanics really is a money-saving pastime.

Many of the courses run for two years, starting with basics and progressing to such advanced subjects as clutch changes and engine overhauls.

For further details, contact your local evening institute office.

Better Driving

Also spreading are Better Driving Courses, staged by road safety units in the boroughs. These are designed to carry on from where the L-schools leave off; indeed they cover a lot of ground that driving instructors don't.

One of the most impressive schemes is run by the London Borough of Greenwich. The Institute of Advanced Motorists supervize the practical on-the-road tests which take place on Sundays. Midweek evening sessions are a mixture of illustrated lectures and written exercises, supplemented by roadwork.

Particular emphasis is placed on night and motorway driving, observation, attitude and basic maintenance checks.

The syllabus also includes: putting the Highway Code into practice; avoiding accidents by concentration; thinking before acting; exercising restraint; driving with deliberation; overtaking; using speed intelligently; developing car sense; reducing mechanical wear and tear; using horn, signals and headlamps thoughtfully; ensuring that the vehicle is roadworthy; perfecting roadcraft; encouraging courtesy; and instilling the system of car control.

First aid courses

One other evening class well worth considering is the special one-off, two-hour First Aid course for motorists, run by the St John Ambulance Brigade. Unlike some European nations — West Germany among them — Britain has been lazy as far as this vital aspect of social responsibility is concerned. Indeed it is law in Germany for every motorist to carry a First Aid kit — and prove they can use it in the driving test.

On the subject of First Aid kits, don't waste your money. Half the objects contained in the average pre-packed kit you'll never use. All you need, insists the St John Ambulance Brigade, are a dozen triangular bandages, two boxes of paper tissues, safety pins, scissors and large adhesive dressings.

But having an emergency kit is one thing. Knowing how to put it to use is another. This is what you'll learn on the special course:

Keeping the airways clear: Moving the head in such a way that obstructed air passages are opened, allowing an accident victim to breathe.

Resuscitation: The next step will be to prepare the casualty — usually a life-like dummy — for mouth-to-mouth resuscitation by shifting position to the left of the patient's head and, still supporting the nape of his neck, tilting his head back. Then, keeping the victim's head extended, you will be asked to open your mouth wide and take a deep breath.

You will then be shown how to pinch the patient's nostrils with your fingers and how to seal your lips around his mouth. After that you simply blow and you'll see his chest rise. Then you take your mouth away and watch his chest deflate. If it were a real patient, you would keep repeating this simple operation until he was able to breathe for himself.

Other things you will be taught will be to remove obstructions at the back of the throat, how to place a patient in the recovery position, and how to pack a deep wound to prevent bleeding.

If what you learn saves only one human life some time in the future, it will have been money well spent. Go along to any St John Ambulance Brigade branch. They'll be pleased to see you.

Self-help

Probably the two most important attributes to safe driving are keeping yourself in good physical shape, and ensuring that you are mentally fit for the task every time you use the car.

First class physical co-ordination is a vital requirement for quick and correct reactions to driving situations: all motorists should see well, hear well, and have good depth perception and night vision.

So have your condition and eyesight checked regularly by your doctor and optician. No driver can afford a sudden disabling attack or seizure. And a motorist convalescing from an illness should always remember that he or she will tire quickly, and should therefore restrict driving to short periods only.

The car on holiday

When good weather persuades thousands of motorists to take to the roads a common cry from those who soon find themselves broken-down is 'My engine has overheated'.

Two main causes are slipping fanbelts and leaking hoses. Both are items that, if the vehicles are looked over before setting out, can be discovered . . . and remedied. Instead, many motorists tend to simply load up, press the starter button and drive away.

What for many promises to be a vacation to remember suddenly becomes a holiday to forget.

Don't let it happen to you. Flick back the pages of this book to page 40 in good time before your departure and follow the checklist right through to page 81. If you're going abroad, take the precaution of packing in some extra spares. The AA and some garages offer comprehensive kits for a small hiring fee. Then, when you return, you pay for any items you may have used.

Just consider that some parts can cost up to four times as much as they do at home because for one thing, sterling is weaker than several Continental currencies.

Bear in mind, too, that motoring abroad can be significantly more demanding on your vehicle than at home. Inevitably longer journeys and, frequently, higher temperatures increase the strain on the cooling, clutch, braking and fuel systems. The steeper gradients can also be extremely demanding. And all that extra luggage can impose a lot more effort on the engine, suspension and tyres.

Also remember that a breakdown on foreign soil can be a great deal more expensive and inconvenient in Britain. In fact, you could save yourself a lot of heartache by taking the simple precaution before you leave of writing a letter to your car's manufacturer to find out where garages which stock your particular make are situated on your proposed journey.

The chances are good that they will stock any spares that may be needed and have the experience and tools to repair the trouble. But it is still very much in your interest to ensure that your instructions are understood and that you request a written estimate of the likely bill before the mechanic starts work.

Any arguments over the cost should be settled *before* you return home; it is virtually impossible to obtain satisfaction once you have departed a foreign country.

Also, before you head for the ferry on the outward trip, seek advice on the type of petrol sold in the country or countries that you plan to visit. The fuel may have a lower lead content than in Britain and could damage your engine unless it is correctly adjusted.

Sleep-driving

And, once on the move, will you be joining the increasing army of holiday motorists who, eager to avoid the Saturday traffic jams, will leave home on Friday evening and do the trip overnight? Even though you have just finished a full day at work? The commonsense answer should be 'No!'. For though you may not realise it, it will be the most dangerous drive of your life.

Studies have brought some experts to the conclusion that 80 per cent of holiday motorists are a menace at night. It is between midnight and 4 am that drivers' reactions are at their most sluggish. So much so that the flicker of trees and the variations of shades of darkness are enough to destroy judgement of speed, distance and timing.

Fatigue is a contributory factor in a large number of accidents and drivers take chances that they wouldn't take if they were alert. This is especially true if you are towing a caravan. You'd be well advised to break your journey and spend the rest of the night in a lay-by.

Things wouldn't be so bad if only motorists took frequent breaks for rest and refreshment — vital during a long night drive. The trouble is that they don't.

To quote a garage owner on a major holiday route: 'Often, while filling up, late-night holiday drivers have told me they have come straight from work without a break. Many are too tired to talk properly, and some have even found it difficult to stand after getting out of their cars. Incredibly, when I have invited them to pull round the side for a rest, they have refused. They say that they want to drive on . . .'

This remarkable 'get there in one hop at all costs' attitude is apparent in daylight, too — especially on long motorway journeys. As a result, a driver's neck suffers because, concentrating on the traffic ahead, he holds his head in an uncomfortable position without realizing it. And this, in turn, instinctively tenses the surrounding muscles which become stiff and painful. All of which is scarcely conducive to safety.

Roof rack loading

Arrange your luggage carefully to minimize wind resistance (1) Better still,

cover the luggage; first laying cover in place, then the largest cases at the bottom and the others in size

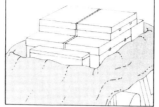

order towards the back (2). Bring cover flaps over, starting with the front, and secure with a 'spider' (3).

Indeed, according to medical scientists, motorway motorists should stop for five minutes in every hour to take a brisk walk and light refreshment. Some countries on the European mainland have actually put up small exercise centres at intervals along main roads.

Caravans and the law

If towing a caravan, the trailer by law must be roadworthy. This means at least one major service a year and, to make sure all is well, a safety check by an expert. That caravan maintenance leaves much to be desired is amply demonstrated in Germany which subjects trailers to a yearly MOT-type test: the failure rate is an amazing 60 per cent.

If you're wise, you will also fit a safety chain – compulsory in some European mainland countries. The device applies the caravan's brakes should the trailer break away from the car.

When touring in the UK, remember the law governing the speed. The maximum is 50 mph – providing the caravan has a '50' sticker on the back, that the gross weight of the caravan does not exceed the kerbside weight of the car, and that the weights are displayed clearly on the nearside of both vehicles. Otherwise 40 mph is the legal maximum.

If going abroad, don't forget to pack a red warning triangle in the boot. If you break down, you must place it well to the rear of the car or caravan.

When loading a caravan, do not make it nose or tail heavy. Put very heavy items over the axle.

Holiday insurance

One of the best holiday insurance schemes if heading abroad, is the AA's 5-Star Travel Scheme. Its benefits include: a-get-you-and-the-car-back-home service in the event of a breakdown, a hired car in which to continue your holiday while your vehicle is off the road, generous medical expenses, and a flying ambulance back to Britain if necessary.

Other suggestions

Be budget-conscious. Planning your route, for instance, can save petrol. And if you're holidaying on the Continent, be courteous – by altering your headlamps to dip to the right side of the road, even though it is not a legal requirement. Fitting lens converters, which clip on to your lights, is the easiest method.

One last precaution: find out beforehand what the speed limits are in the countries you will visit, and how their motoring laws differ from ours.

Their embassies in this country will be able to help.

Hiring a car

To prevent wear and tear on your own vehicle, you may be considering hiring a car instead. If you do, shop around for the best deal. Try and calculate your mileage in advance and get the hire companies to provide you with an estimate in advance, so you know just how much everything will work out to.

If hiring for Continental driving, it will probably work out cheaper to lease the car abroad. By using such international firms as Hertz or Avis, however, you will be able to make arrangements this side of the channel – and pay in sterling.

If you also intend hiring a caravan, seek the advice of the Caravan Club (see below) or a major manufacturer like CI (Caravans International) of The Oaks, Fordham Road, Newmarket, Cambridgeshire.

For hiring of camping equipment, contact Black and Edgington at Ruxley Corner, Sidcup, Kent.

Useful addresses:

British Tourist Authority, 64 St James's Street, London SW1 (01-629 9191). Caravan Club of Great Britain, East Grinstead, Sussex (East Grinstead 26944).

Road organiz- ations

There are two principal road organizations in Britain:
The Royal Automobile Club,
83–85 Pall Mall,
London SW1 (01-930 4343),
and
The Automobile Association,
Fanum House,
Basingstoke, Hants.
(Basingstoke 20123).

Services

Both organizations, in return for an annual membership subscription, offer:
Free Breakdown Service by skilled mobile patrols, or appointed garages, equipped to carry out minor roadside repairs. In the event of failing to get the member going, the patrol will tow or low-load the car and its occupants to the nearest available appointed garage. The garage mechanic will tow or low-load the car and its occupants to his base.

For an additional subscription a member, in the event of a breakdown or accident is entitled to have his vehicle and occupants taken to his home or any mainland destination (RAC). The AA scheme does not cover accidents, but does include ferrying of caravans and trailers.

There are more than 1400 AA and RAC telephone points at selected roadside locations, access to which can be gained by a member's key, regardless of which organization he belongs to. Assistance can also be summoned from public call boxes and motorway emergency telephones.

The basic subscription also entitles members to:

Technical services which provide information on all technical matters. Help and advice is also available in cases of dispute with manufacturers or garages, provided that cases are supported by invoices and other relevant documents.
(For an additional fee, examinations of vehicles prior to purchase or for any other reason can be carried out by experienced engineers.)

Legal services which provide free advice and information, and free legal representation in cases of motoring offences in courts of summary jurisdiction or their equivalent. Free advice is also given on claims against other parties arising out of accidents.

Insurance services which provide free quotations, advice and information.

Travel services which provide free information on all aspects of touring in Britain and, if desired, route advice for any journey in the UK and on the European mainland. Individual requirements (country routes, scenic tours and routes avoiding traffic bottlenecks and steep hills) are also supplied.

Personal loan schemes which carry specially negotiated rates of interest for members.

In addition, both organizations run their own travel agencies; and hotel, guest house, restaurant, caravan site and camping site classification schemes.

The AA also has a classification scheme for its approved garages, a members' mail order service, a spares kit service, and *Drive* magazine which has

earned a high reputation for its in-depth investigations and consumer crusades.

Both organizations also produce an excellent handbook with maps and a comprehensive gazeteer.

Main regional headquarters of the AA are:
South-East Region, Fanum House, 7 High Street, Teddington, Middlesex TW11 8EQ
01-977 3200
Midlands Region, Fanum House, Dogkennel Lane, Halesowen, West Midlands B63 3BT
021-550 4721
North Region, Fanum House, Station Road, Cheadle Hulme, Cheadle, Cheshire SK8 7BS
061-485 6188
Wales and West Region, Fanum House, Park Row, Bristol BS1 5LY
0272-297 272
Scotland and N. Ireland Region, Erskine Harbour, Erskine, Renfrewshire PA8 6AT
041-812 0144
Republic of Ireland, AA Headquarters, 23 Suffolk 23 Suffolk Street, Dublin 2 Dublin 779481
Main provincial RAC offices are:
Southern Home Counties, Lansdowne Road, Croydon.
Northern Home Counties, St Albans Road, Watford.
South-West Counties, 4-6 White Ladies Road, Bristol.
Western Counties, 15-17 Union Street, Plymouth.
Midlands Counties, 93-95 Hagley Road, Edgbaston, Birmingham.
North-West Counties, 135 Dickenson Road, Manchester.
Scotland (Eastern Counties), 17 Rutland Square, Edinburgh.
Scotland (Western Counties), 242 West George Street, Glasgow.

Know your tyres

See how many of the following questions you can get right without looking at your car or handbook . . .

1. What size are the tyres fitted to your car?

2. Are they cross-ply, textile radial, or steel-braced radial?

3. What are the recommended pressures?

4. Which is correct: 'When mixing tyres, cross-plys should go on the front and radials on the rear' or: 'Radials should go on the front and cross-plys on the rear'?

5. What is the legal maximum length of a cut exposing cords in a tyre wall?

The answers to questions 4 and 5 are at the foot of the page. How well did you get on? The chances are: not very well. For when these same posers were put to 100 motorists in a recent survey, only 13 knew the size of their tyres, 30 the answer to the fourth Question, and 10 the answer to Question 5.

It is a remarkable fact that, though tyres are a driver's sole contact with the road, the average motorist knows very little about them. He needs to . . . for there are any number of rogues at scrap merchants and backstreet dealers all too willing to take advantage of the situation. Remember: it's YOUR safety that's at stake. The figures and symbols on the side wall indicate the size of the tyres.

Cross-ply tyres

In addition to the brand name, you will notice some figures with a letter in between. These may read something like: 6.40S13, or 6.2S12, or 9.5S14.

The figures on the left-hand side of the letter denote the nominal section width of the tyre – in other words the measurement from centre wall to centre wall. The numbers on the right of the letter tell you the wheel diameter on to which the tyre fits. So, if the code is 6.40S13, the nominal section width of the tyre is 6.4ins, and the wheel diameter to which the tyre fits is 13ins.

The letter, S, stands for 'Standard'. This, in fact, is a speed rating. And in the case of a 13 in diameter wheel and over, the 'S' means that the maximum speed capabilities of the car to which the tyre may be fitted is 110mph. On a rim diameter of 12in, the 'S' stands for 100mph; and on a 10in, 95mph.

There are two other letter symbols – H (high speed) and V (very high speed). On a 10in rim, H=110mph; V=over 110 mph. On a 12in rim, H=115 mph; V=over 115mph. And on a 13in rim, H=125mph; V=over 125mph.

Radial tyres

On radial tyres, the numbers and letters are slightly different. The letters, S, H and V are suffixed by an R which denotes 'Radial'. The figures on the left are, once again, the nominal section width, but expressed in milli-metres. The numbers on the right, denoting the wheel rim diameter, represent inches as they do on cross-plys. Thus, 165SR14, means a 'Standard' radial tyre with a nominal section width of 165mm on a rim diameter of 14in. Regardless of the rim diameter, the maximum speed capabilities of the car to which the tyre may be fitted are: SR=113mph, HR=130mph,

VR=over 130mph.

Even though the legal maximum speed in Britain is 70mph (and then on motor-ways), you may not fit an SR tyre on a car that is capable of, say, 125mph. It must have HR tyres, and an observant police officer could book you if you erred.

Another tyre type is the '70 Series', so called because its section height is 70 per cent of the section width. Such models incorporate the number 70 preceded by millimetric or code markings.

Ensure that a dealer fits the correct tyres to your car by referring to the code recom-mended in your car handbook. When new tyres are fitted – whether remoulds or brand-new – run them in. Do not exceed 50mph for the first 100 miles.

Tread patterns

Tyre manufacturers produce a variety of tread patterns for different conditions and usage. So when buying replacements, seek the advice of the dealer on the best type for your requirements. Chunky winter tread tyres, for example, are perfect in mud and snow, but unsuitable for high-speed motoring because the thick tread generates excessive heat which can cause failure.

For further information on tyres, refer to the Book list on page 91, and to the National Tyre Distributors Association, Broadway House, Broadway, London SW19 (01-540 3859).

Answers: 4. The first statement is correct; 5. One inch or 10 per cent of a tyre's section width, whichever is the greater.

Accidents

If you are wise, you will have a piece of paper on the front parcel-shelf already marked with 10 headlines and with space under each one. Hopefully, you will never need to use it – because it will be an accident report form.

However much you believe that it could never happen to you, drivers, statistically, are likely to be involved in an accident of some kind every seven years. And in the confusion, in the shock of the moment if and when it does happen, vital details don't always register in the mind. So that when you come to fill in the relevant insurance form, you're not at all sure what really happened.

Record the facts in writing as soon as possible after the collision, and your recollections will be much clearer.

These are the headlines you will need to have:

1. Names and addresses of eyewitnesses.
2. The make and model of the other vehicle.
3. Its colour.
4. Its registration number.
5. The name and address of its driver.
6. A description of the other driver (height, physical characteristics, clothes, distinguishing marks etc.).
7. The other driver's insurance details.
8. The condition of the road (wet, dry, icy).
9. What happened (give a full account).

10. Sketch map of the accident location, showing the attitude of the vehicles immediately before and after the impact. Mark any road markings, signs, etc.

Of course, you will have to amend the headlines accordingly if the other party is a pedestrian.

The other golden rules to remember are:

* Never admit liability – you could be in breach of the conditions of your policy.
* Never offer to pay for damage – this could be construed as an admission of liability.
* Inform your insurance company within the time period stated on the policy.
* Report the accident, however slight, to the police within 24 hours.

The law demands that you *must* stop if the accident involves another person or vehicle. It is also a legal requirement that you supply your name and address and your car's registration number to anyone involved in the mishap who asks for them.

In the event of someone being injured, it is mandatory to produce your insurance certificate so the details can be noted. And if the car you are driving belongs to someone else, you must give the name and address of its owner.

When reporting the matter to the police, you will probably be asked to produce your insurance certificate within five days. Remember, too, that it is essential to inform the police if you run over a dog.

There are two other eventualities which must be reported to the police – the failure of another driver involved to stop. And if, for any reason, another driver involved refuses to supply his name and address when you ask for them.

Vehicle recovery

If, after an accident, you are unfit to drive (asuming that your car is still driveable), the police will arrange for a garage to collect the vehicle.

Insurance details

If your policy and that of the other driver are comprehensive, it is usual for each insurer to pay for the damage of the policy-holder's vehicle, regardless of who was to blame.

At some point, you will have to decide whether to make an insurance claim, or to pay the repair costs out of your own pocket. Paying up yourself could be the lesser of two evils if the combined sum of the voluntary damage excess and whatever percentage of your no-claim discount will be lost works out to more than the claim. If in doubt, ask your insurance broker's advice.

Be careful because, these days, the size of the rises in the cost of insurance premiums can increase the penalty substantially.

If you take the car abroad, seek your broker's advice on the extra cover you may require. And if you are towing a caravan, mention the fact.

If you plan to visit Spain or Spanish territory, make sure you get a bail bond from your insurance company. In the event of an accident, Spanish courts have a habit of demanding a surety for bail and security against any fine that might later be imposed. Without a bail bond, you could be imprisoned and your vehicle impounded until a trial.

Any other queries you may have should be directed to your broker, insurance company, or the British Insurance Association at:
Aldermary House,
Queen Street,
London EC4 (01-248 4477).

Book list

HISTORY

The Light Car, (a technical history), C F Caunter, Her Majesty's Stationery Office, 1970, £1.25.
Technical history of cars with engines of less than 1600cc capacity from the late 19th century to the present, and a glimpse into the future.

Automobile Design, Ronald Barker and Anthony Harding, David and Charles, 1973, £3.25.
Biographies of 11 pioneering automobile engineers with emphasis on their design work and achievements.

Bosch Book of the Motor Car, John Day, William Collins, 1975, £4.95.
How the various parts that make up the motor car were invented and developed. The text traces the history from the 18th century steamers to present-day models and beyond.

World Cars, Automobile Club of Italy, Herald, 1975, £7.50.
Specifications and pictures of current production models world-wide, with details of manufacturers, outputs etc.

MAINTENANCE

New Motor Manual,
edited by Leonard Holmes, Hamlyn, 1970, £1.50.
Comprehensive guide to the modern car's mechanism, maintenance, overhaul and general operation. Written by nine expert contributors, the accent is on British and imported cars of recent years, and the book is packed with information for the D-I-Y owner.

The Car Doctor A – Z,
B C Macdonald, Elliot Right Way Books, 1970, 40p.
ABC fault-finder, covering symptoms, causes and cures. A precise step-by-step guide of what to do in every circumstance, routine and emergency.

Car Repairs Properly Explained, B C Macdonald, Elliot Right Way Books, 1970, 40p.
How to reduce the cost of running a car by doing your own maintenance and, as far as possible, your own repairs. Special emphasis on electrical faults. Plus a chapter on decarbonizing, and an oil chart for every model of car.

The Mechanism of The Car,
A W Judge, Chapman and Hall, 1966, £3.75 each.
Series of eight comprehensive manuals on: 1 Automobile Engines, 2 Carburettors and Fuel Injection Systems, 3 Mechanisms of The Car, 4 Car Maintenance and Repairs, 5 Modern Transmission Systems, 6 Modern Electric Equipment for Automobiles, 7 Modern Smaller Diesel Engines, 8 Automobile Brakes and Braking Systems.

MOTORING

Driving Manual, Her Majesty's Stationery Office, 1972, £1.15.
Authoritative guide for those who take their driving seriously, showing how standards can be kept up and improved on.

AA Guide to Used Cars,
Automobile Association, 1975, £1.75 (£1.50 to AA members).
Fifty popular models, and the faults likely to occur in any of the years covered. Also hints on prices throughout the country.

AA Book of the Car,
Automobile Association, Drive Publications, 1974, £8.95 (£7.95 to AA members).
A brilliantly illustrated volume which covers motoring history, how a car works, tools, faults and maintenance, accessories, motoring costs, driving fitness and better driving.

Lucas Make the L Test Easy,
Roy Johnstone, Foulsham, 1976, 95p.
A manual that prepares the novice for professional driving tuition with 'in-car' instruction indoors and out. A guide for the future standard European driving test, it also includes sections on maintenance and first aid. There are also rating tests and a special chart which monitors an L school pupil's progress.

AA Touring Guides to . . .
England, Wales, Scotland, Ireland, Automobile Association, 1975 and 1976, £6.45 each (£4.95 to AA members).
Lavishly illustrated works containing day drive selections, gazeteer, and feature articles on customs, traditions, house styles etc.

AA Illustrated Guide to Britain, Automobile Association, Drive Publications, 1974, £8.95 (£7.95 to AA members.
Richly-illustrated, detailed gazeteer. It divides the country into 190 different touring regions, which are described by authors with soft spots for the locations highlighted.

What Car? Haymarket Publishing Ltd., Regent House, 54-62 Regent St., London W1A 4YJ, 35p.

Motoring Which?
Consumers' Association, 14 Buckingham St., London WC2N 6DS. By subscription or through libraries.

Glossary

Accelerator: Pedal by which the engine speed is controlled.

Additives: Chemicals and other agents added to petrol and oil to provide increased efficiency.

Air-cooled engine: Engine that is directly cooled by air usually blown by a fan over finned cylinder heads.

Air filter: Device mounted on the air intake of the carburettor to prevent dirt and dust from entering the engine.

Alternator: Generator that produces alternating current, and a higher power output than a dynamo at low engine speeds.

Ammeter: Dashboard instrument which measures the amount of current to or from the battery.

Anti-burst lock: Mechanism which prevents a door from opening in a collision,

Antifreeze: Chemical additive which, when mixed with water in the cooling system, prevents ice formation in temperatures below 0 degrees centigrade.

Anti-roll bar: Steel torsion bar whose winding-up action on corners prevents roll motion.

Aquaplaning: Build-up of water under the tyres that induces a skating effect and makes steering impossible.

Armature: Revolving component of an electric motor or generator.

Automatic choke: Pre-set carburettor mechanism that automatically produces a rich mixture when the engine is cold and a normal mixture when the engine is warm.

Automatic transmission: Gearbox that automatically selects the correct gear ratio for the vehicle's speed and road gradients.

Axle: Component that carries the roadwheels.

Backfire: An explosion in the exhaust usually caused by a leak in the system, retarded ignition, or a weak mixture.

Ball bearings: Rows of steel balls that rotate between rings and support a revolving shaft or wheel on a fixed shaft.

Ball joint: Coupling which allows two components to pivot in any direction relative to the other.

Bevel gear: Conical-shaped gears that transmit motion from one shaft to another often through an angle of 90 degrees.

Big end: Larger end of a connecting rod joined to the crank-pin of the crankshaft.

Bleeding: Expulsion of air through a nipple from a sealed hydraulic or cooling system.

Bore: The diameter of a cylinder.

Brake fade: Loss of braking efficiency through overheating.

Brake horsepower: A measure of a vehicle's power output.

Breather: Vent allowing air pressure to be equalized in an otherwise enclosed chamber.

Brushes: Pads in contact with a commutator and which receive current from a dynamo armature, or supply current to an electric motor armature.

Cadence braking: Pumping the brake pedal in harmony with suspension motion to prevent locking-up of the rear wheels.

Camber angle: Angle of tilt of a car's road-wheels.

Camshaft: Shaft driven by and which runs at half the speed of the crankshaft. It operates the inlet and exhaust valves for each cylinder.

Carburettor: The component that supplies a mixture of petrol and air to the engine to suit the operating conditions.

Charge: The battery's current input from the dynamo or alternator.

Childproof lock: Mechanism which prevents a car door from being opened from inside.

Choke: Carburettor device that ensures a richer petrol and air mixture when starting a cold engine.

Clutch: Mechanical device that connects and disconnects the engine from the transmission.

Coil: Transformer that provides the high voltage to produce sparks for combustion.

Combustion: Ignition by spark of the petrol-air mixture after the action of the piston has compressed the gas in the cylinder.

Condenser: Distributor device that reduces the tendency of the contact-breaker points to burn.

Constant-mesh gears: The gears in a gearbox that are in mesh at all times.

Crankshaft: Shaft that, through connecting rods, converts the up and down motion of the pistons into a rotary action.

Damper: Suspension shock absorber.

Differential gear: Gear system in the final drive that enables the powered roadwheels to revolve at different speeds.

Distributor: Component that sends high voltage current from the coil to the sparking plugs in turn.

Dynamo: Engine-driven generator that produces direct current.

Electrolyte: Solution of acid and water in a battery.

Electronic ignition: Device that produces high-voltage sparks for high-revving engines.

Electronic fuel injection: Device that controls fuel delivery depending on inlet manifold suction, engine rpm and temperature, and accelerator position.

Flat spot: Hesitant engine response at a particular throttle opening.

Flywheel: Weighty toothed disc connected to the crankshaft.

Full lock: Limit of steering-wheel travel.

Gaiters: Synthetic rubber bellows that prevent dirt and grit entering moving parts, and lubricant escaping.

Gasket: Leak-proof seal between two mating surfaces.

Grommet: Rubber plug fitted to a panel to prevent leakage, noise, or cable chafing.

Half-shafts: Axles that transmit the drive from the differential gear to the roadwheels.

Hunting: Erratic engine running usually caused by a weak fuel mixture.

Jet: Device in a carburettor that ensures correct fuel flow.

Knocking: Metallic noise caused by excessively rapid burning of the petrol/air mixture in the combustion chamber.

Manifold: Pipe or passage system in a casting with several openings.

Misfire: Erratic running of engine caused by a cylinder failing to fire.

Negative earth: Negative battery terminal earthed to car's structure.

Overdrive: Supplementary gearbox, electrically controlled, designed to improve fuel consumption.

Oversteer: Reduction in the amount of steering lock in order to remain on intended course.

Piston rings: Thin metal bands which fit in grooves around the pistons to form seals against the cylinder walls.

Points: Distributor contact breaker points which open and shut as the crankshaft rotates and make and break the ignition circuit to cause a spark at the sparking plug.

Push rods: Camshaft-driven rods that open and shut the engine's valves in an overhead-valve system.

Rotary engine: Engine in which the motion producing power is rotary instead of reciprocal.

Servo: Device that uses the suction effort of the inlet manifold to reduce the amount of pedal effort when operating the footbrake.

Short engine: Reconditioned engine not including cylinder head and accessories.

Suppressor: Device that prevents a car's electrical system from interfering with radio and TV reception.

Synchromesh: Manual gearbox device that synchronizes the speeds of two gearwheels, making gearchanging easier.

Tappets: Hard metal blocks pushed up by cams on the camshaft to operate the engine valves.

Understeer: Increase in the amount of steering lock in order to remain on intended course.

Wheelbase: The distance between the front and rear axles with the steering straight.

Index

Credits

Artists
Terry Allen Associates Ltd.
Diagram
Ron Hayward Art Group
David Lewis Management

Photographs:
British Leyland: Contents, 16, 17
Colin Taylor Productions: 60
Compagnie Française de Pétroles: 32
Ferrari: Contents, 34
Ford Archives: 10
Ford (UK): 17

John Topham Picture Library: 27, 28
London Arts Technical: 29
Mansell Collection: 4, 7
Mercedes-Benz: 6
Messerschmitt: 15
Peter Myers: 38, 70
National Motor Museum: Contents, 9, 11, 29, 31
B. P. Price: 27
Radio Times Hulton Picture Library: 26, 27, 28, 30, 31
Robert Hunt Library: 11
Veteran Car Club of Great Britain: 26
Volvo: 16